Cisco VIRL Hands-on Lab Guide
Network Simulation Workbook

Version 1.0

- ➤ Get Proficient with Cisco VIRL
- ➤ Build CCNA, CCNP and CCIE Level Labs
- ➤ Real-world Scenarios Mock-up
- ➤ Step-by-step and Easy-to-follow Guide

SPEAK NETWORK
SOLUTIONS

Speak Network Solutions – www.speaknetworks.com

© 2018, Speak Network Solutions, LLC. All rights reserved.

You may only use this Documentation as a reference manual for your personal use. You may not, in whole or in part, copy, distribute, display, modify, use any part of a compilation or create a derivative work of this Documentation.

Disclaimer

The information provided in this document is provided "as is" without warranty of any kind. Speak Network Solutions disclaims all warranties, either express or implied, including the warranties of merchantability and fitness for a particular purpose. In no event shall Speak Network Solutions be liable for any damages whatsoever including direct, indirect, incidental, consequential damages, including but not limited to procurement of substitute goods or services, loss of data, loss of profits, and/or business interruptions, even if Speak Network Solutions or its suppliers have been advised of the possibility of such damages.

The Documentation may contain "links" to sites on the Internet that are not created by, or under the control of Speak Network Solutions. Such links are provided solely for your convenience. Speak Network Solutions assumes no responsibility for the availability or content of such other sites.

The opinions expressed in this guide are those of the author and are not necessarily those of Cisco Systems, Inc. The author is not affiliated with Cisco Systems, Inc.

The trademarks that are used are without any consent, and the publication of the trademark is without permission or backing by the trademark owner. All trademarks and brands within this guide are for clarifying purposes only and are the property of the owners themselves and are not affiliated with this document.

Resources

For your convenience, code scripts, sample configuration files and network diagrams and topologies covered in this guide are available and can be downloaded. Please refer to www.speaknetworks.com for the most current information. Training articles and videos including samples are added periodically. Please sign up newsletter on the website to receive email updates.

Where to get help

Documentation, release notes, software updates, and information about Speak Network Solutions products, licensing, and services, are at Speak Network Solutions' website at:

>   https://www.speaknetworks.com

Your comments

Your suggestions will help us continue to improve the accuracy, organization, and overall quality of the publications. Please send your opinion of this document to:

>   info@speaknetworks.com

ISBN-13: 978-1722958633

ISBN-10: 1722958634

Table of Contents

Introduction 4

Lab Environment Preparation 7

Topology 1: VLAN, Trunking, STP and Ether-Channel 17

Topology 2: Configuring EIGRP IPv4 and IPv6 32

Topology 3: Configuring OSPF IPv4 and IPv6 42

Topology 4: Configuring IOS NAT/PAT 53

Topology 5: Configuring ASA with Multiple DMZ Networks (Security) 63

Topology 6: Configuring L2TP Over IPSec VPN on Cisco ASA (Security) 78

Topology 7: Configuring Automatic ISP Failover (WAN, BGP) 89

Topology 8: Configuring DMVPN With IPSec and EIGRP Overlay 110

Topology 9: Configuring MPLS VPN, VRF, OSPF and BGP 127

Appendix A: Using External Telnet SSH Clients 140

Appendix B: Node Naming and IP Addressing Scheme 145

Appendix C: Recommended Reading 148

Introduction

Purpose

The purpose of this workbook is to guide you through configuring and testing common network topologies using Cisco VIRL. The knowledge and proficiency acquired after completing the examples in this workbook will help you in preparing CCNA, CCNP and CCIE level exams, as well as in administrating and configuring real-world networking environment.

The information and configuration examples provided in the workbook are for academic and educational purposes only. They shall not be used in production environment without thorough testing and validations. Speak Network Solutions assumes no responsibility for any loss or hardship caused directly or indirectly by using of its contents.

About Cisco VIRL

Cisco Virtual Internet Routing Lab (VIRL) is a software tool Cisco developed to build and run network simulations without the need for physical hardware.

Under the hood, VIRL is an OpenStack-based platform that runs IOSv, IOSv Layer-2, IOS-XRv, NX-OSv, CSR1000v and ASAv software images on the built-in hypervisor. VIRL provides a scalable, extensible network design and simulation environment using the VM Maestro client and web GUI. VIRL also has extensive ability to integrate with third-party virtual machines, appliances, VNFs and servers such as Microsoft Windows, Juniper, Palo Alto Networks, Fortinet, F5, Extreme Networks, Arista, Alcatel, Citrix and more.

Cisco VIRL may also connect with real-world and virtual networks to form high-fidelity development and test environments. More importantly, VIRL and its testing environment are portable. You can export a lab configuration and import into another VIRL server with ease. The key benefits include-

Official Cisco Images

VIRL comes with a complete set of legal and licensed Cisco IOS images that are the same as those running on physical routers (with minor tweaks to optimize them running in a virtual environment). The new Cisco IOS releases are provided in a regular basis.

Runs on Most Computers

The minimum hardware requirement for VIRL is an Intel-based computer with four virtual CPU cores, 8GB of RAM and 70 GB free disk space. VIRL can be installed on laptops, desktops or servers. It can be deployed as a virtual machine in VMware or on bare-metal machines.

Flexible Installation Options

You can install a VIRL on an enterprise-grade server infrastructure, a desktop computer, a laptop, or even on the cloud. You can run it as a Virtual Machine on VMware ESXi, VMware Workstation, Player or VMware Fusion for Mac OS. You may choose to build VIRL on a bare-metal computer as well. Once your VIRL lab is up and running, it is an all-in-one virtual networking lab that has no wires and cords attached. When you run it as a VM, you can scale, migrate and implement high availability (HA) by taking advantage of the features that VMware infrastructure has to offer.

Automatic Configuration

The AutoNetkit, which comes with VIRL, can assign IP addresses to the nodes automatically when they launch, and it will even set up some basic routing protocols for you. The bootstrap configuration gives you a fully converged network as soon as they are launched. And you can go straight to the features and focus on what you want to test. This is a cool feature for network engineers who want to set up a one-time temporary environment to look up commands and test certain features. If you were building a network topology from scratch, or creating a mockup a production environment, manual IP addressing is recommended.

Community Support by Developers

VIRL is supported by a community full of good people like you. Questions are often answered first-hand by developers and engineers. The Cisco VIRL team offers webinars and newsletters to keep the community updated on new feature releases and announcements. You can find the online community on Cisco Learning Network at: https://learningnetwork.cisco.com/groups/virl

For more information, go to Cisco VIRL's website at: http://virl.cisco.com

Prerequisites

This workbook assumes that you have basic knowledge of computer networking. Cisco routers and switches admin experiences would be a plus. The perfect audience would be who are planning to or in the process of pursuing Cisco networking certifications, network engineers working in real-world environment.

A working VIRL server setup, running VIRL 1.3 and later. The VIRL server can be installed on a hypervisor such as VMware ESXi, VMware Workstation for Windows, Fusion Pro for Mac, on a bare-metal computer, or on the Cloud.

> To get started with Cisco VIRL, read about how to acquire a license, prepare and build a server, refer to our in-depth guide - The VIRL BOOK.
>
> http://www.virlbook.com

Finally, you'll need a laptop or a desktop computer. Windows, Mac or Linux with graphical user interface. This computer will be used to access the VIRL server and complete most of the tasks in this workbook.

Lab Environment Preparation

VIRL Networking Overview

Before we start with our labs, it is beneficial to understand how the networking works inside a VIRL server. The VIRL server itself is a KVM-enabled hypervisor, where all the simulated nodes run within. If you were running VIRL on a VMware hypervisor as a VM guest, all of a sudden you have created a two-level deep virtual environment. It is called "Nested Virtualization".

Here is the overall topology of how VIRL, LXC and the simulation work together. Note each node would have their management interface connected to the LXC. The management interface does not participate in data-plane traffic. It is designed for management only. From a user's perspective, we can login either through the management interface or directly over the IP of data network port. The same theory applies to how you access a physical network device. For example, you can choose to manage a Cisco ASA over its management interface or one of its data interfaces.

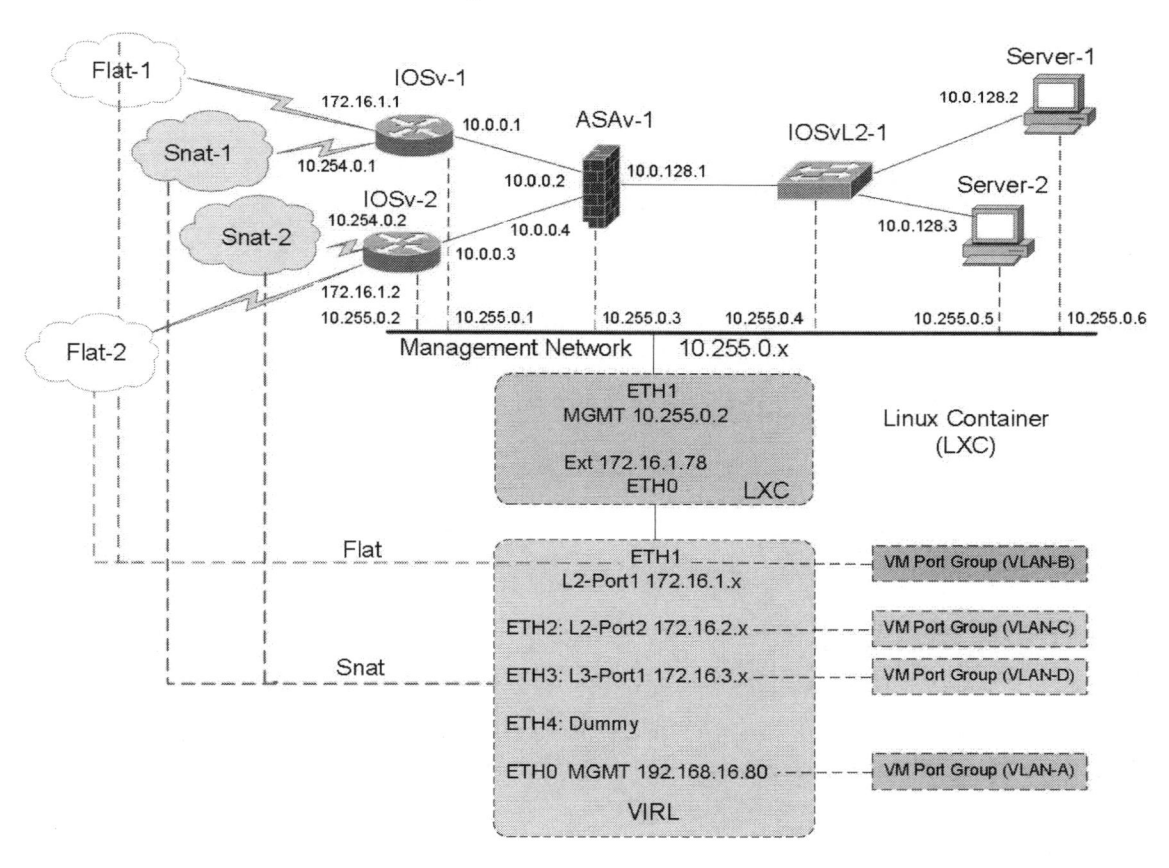

The diagram above represents a "Private" lab. It can be either a Private Project or a Private Simulation. A private network uses LXC, while a "Shared flat network" does not use a LXC.

Private Simulation

- Private Simulation has its own LXC. LXC has connectivity to only those nodes running within a single simulation.

- The LXC cannot see and therefore cannot access the nodes in any other simulations, even those running as part of the same project.

Private Project

- Private Project shares a LXC, even though there are multiple simulations going on in the same Project.

- The LXC cannot see and therefore cannot access the nodes in any other project.

As you can see the LXC is not only used as a convenient jump-box, it is also used to create a barrier to segregate multiple simulations or projects in a shared lab environment.

Shared FLAT Network

- A shared flat network eliminates the needs of a LXC.

- The management interfaces of the nodes in a simulation are placed directly on the FLAT (172.16.1.0/24) network.

- Nodes have visibility to all other nodes in simulations, regardless project or user.

- VIRL will have direct access to all simulated nodes via its ETH1 on the FLAT network.

To change the type of a simulation, click on the blank area of a network topology (without selecting any node) and go to "Properties > Topology". Here you can choose the type from a pull-down menu.

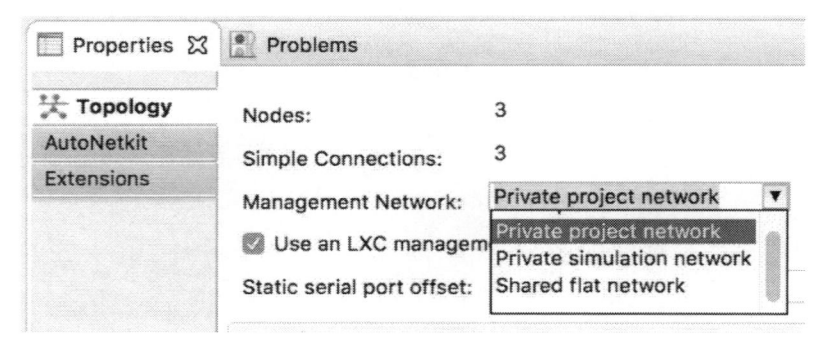

Illustrated below is a Shared FLAT Network. Since we're going to use the FLAT subnet for data-plane connectivity we will have to use one of the "private" methods for management. A FLAT network cannot be used for both management and data-plane connectivity at the same time.

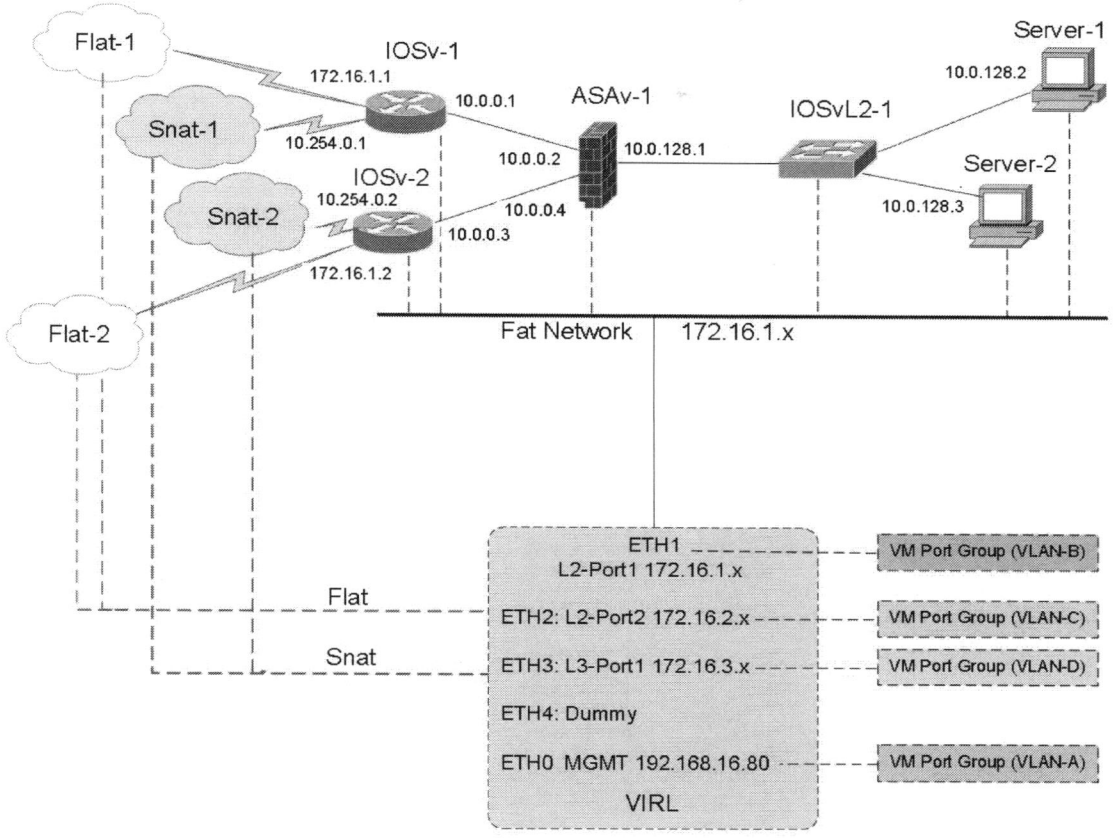

> It is recommended to review the fundamental concepts and knowledge about VIRL before moving on to the labs. The VIRL BOOK covers in-depth knowledge and prepares you for this workbook.
>
> http://www.virlbook.com

Connecting to VIRL Server

When you launch VM Maestro client for the first time, you'll be prompted to enter the VIRL server's IP address. The default username and password are "guest" and "guest". After you logged in, make sure the VM Maestro client is communicating with the VIRL server and that all the web services are running.

Navigate to the menu and click on the "Properties". Select "Web Servers" on the left. This is where the VIRL server IP and ports are configured. There are two sets of ports required - ports used by VM Maestro to communicate with VIRL, and the ports used by the SSH/Telnet client to connect with the Console or management interfaces of the simulated network nodes.

- Web Services: 19399
- Configuration Visualization Port: 19401
- Live Simulation Visualization Port: 19402

Under Web Services, all items should show green "Compatible".

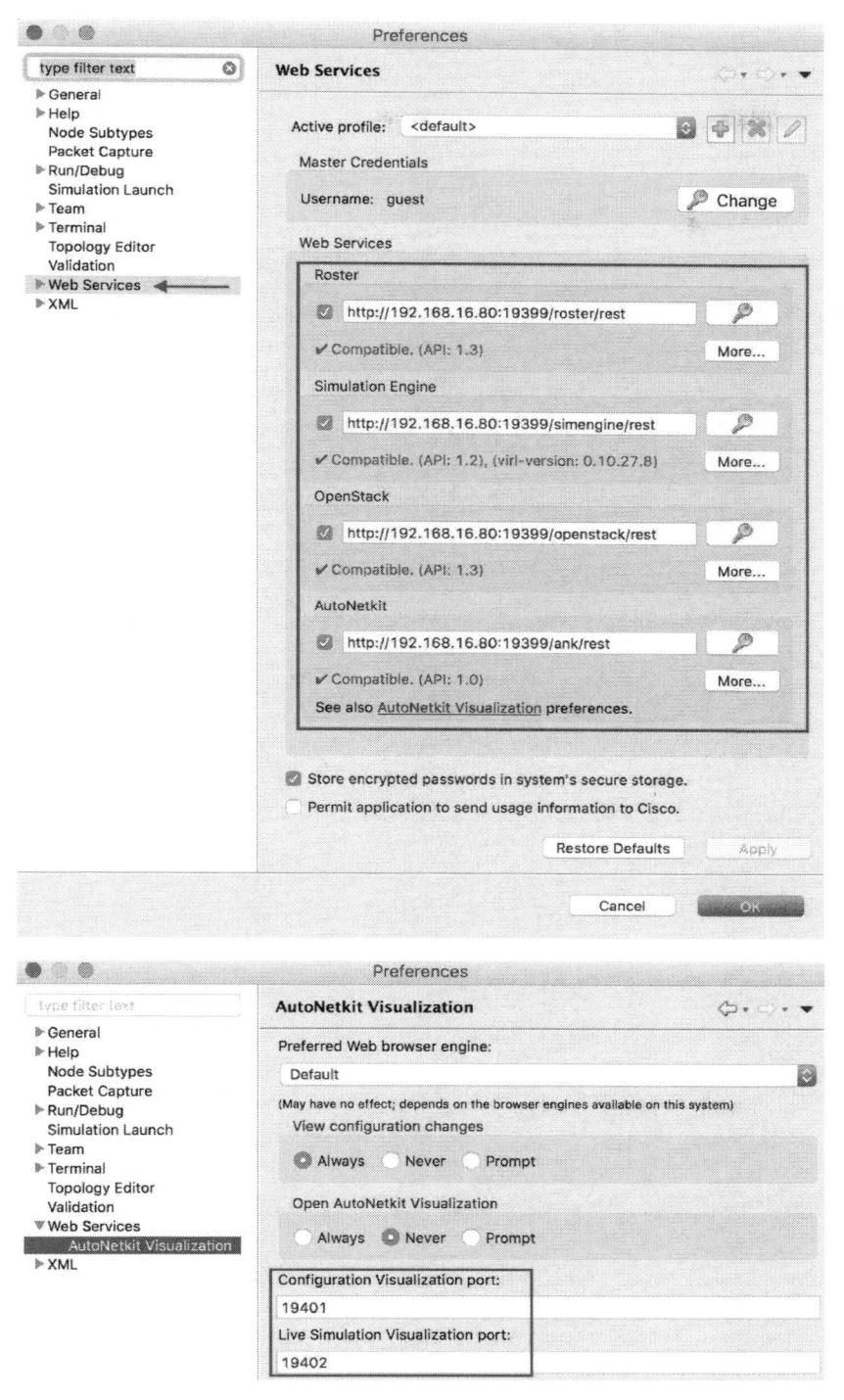

There are two common issues if your VM Maestro client fails to connect. If all items under Web Services are showing "red", make sure you have network connectivity to the VIRL Server and that TCP port "19399" is open. It shouldn't be a problem if you are on the same LAN as the VIRL server. If there was a firewall between the VM Maestro client and the VIRL server, you need to make a firewall rule to allow those three TCP ports

(19399, 19401 and 19402). If only one or two items failed checking, you'll need to troubleshoot the issues on the VIRL server itself before moving forward.

Downloading Workbook Materials

The workbook materials can be downloaded on the author's website. The downloaded files are designed to work together with this workbook. As you work through the labs, code snippets included in the download allow you to copy and paste without having to type in all the code manually.

> **Note:** Before you start the first Lab, be sure to download the workbook materials at:
>
> www.speaknetworks.com

Under each topology folder, there are three files included:

- network diagram.png
- initial.virl
- final.virl

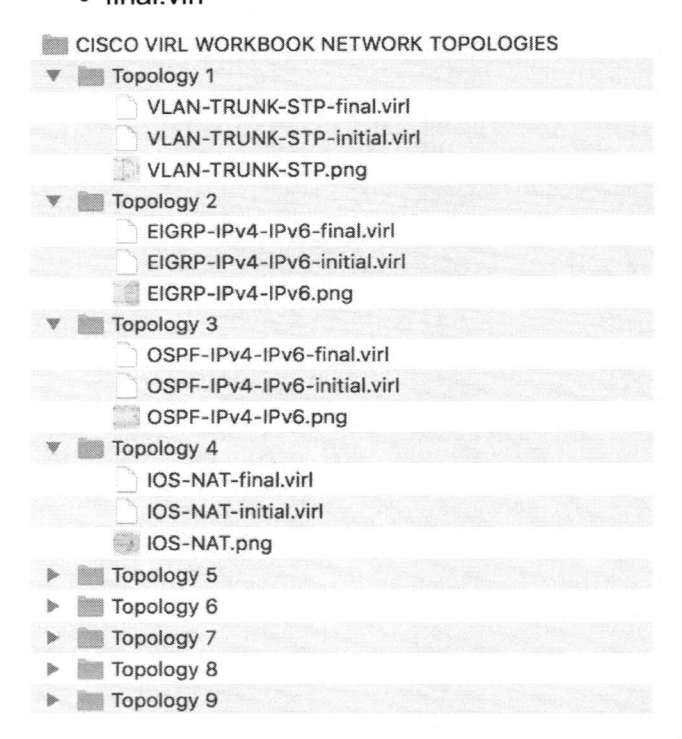

```
CISCO VIRL WORKBOOK NETWORK TOPOLOGIES
▼ Topology 1
      VLAN-TRUNK-STP-final.virl
      VLAN-TRUNK-STP-initial.virl
      VLAN-TRUNK-STP.png
▼ Topology 2
      EIGRP-IPv4-IPv6-final.virl
      EIGRP-IPv4-IPv6-initial.virl
      EIGRP-IPv4-IPv6.png
▼ Topology 3
      OSPF-IPv4-IPv6-final.virl
      OSPF-IPv4-IPv6-initial.virl
      OSPF-IPv4-IPv6.png
▼ Topology 4
      IOS-NAT-final.virl
      IOS-NAT-initial.virl
      IOS-NAT.png
▶ Topology 5
▶ Topology 6
▶ Topology 7
▶ Topology 8
▶ Topology 9
```

The network diagram is a snapshot of a VIRL topology, illustrating how the routers and hosts are interconnected. The "initial.virl" file is a VIRL topology that can be natively imported into VM Maestro client or the web frontend UWM. It includes the basic wiring and IP addressing on all the nodes. As a baseline setup, you may configure the required lab tasks by following along the instructions in this workbook. With the "final.virl" file, it is a fully configured and working VIRL lab satisfying all the requirements in the lab. Therefore, it is the "solution" to each scenario.

Loading Lab Initial Configuration in VM Maestro Client

The "initial.virl" file contains the network topology and baseline configuration on all the nodes in a particular lab. It is to help you save time creating the topology in VM Maestro client if you were to do it from scratch by yourself. It is optional, you could choose to build it without using the initial file, however.

> **Note:** This workbook assumes that you use the "initial.virl" baseline topology and node configuration since all nodes use static IP addresses. See **Appendix B: Node Naming and IP Addressing Scheme**.

To load the initial configuration files, launch VM Maestro client, go to "File > Import". Select "Import topology file(s) from local file system" and click "Next".

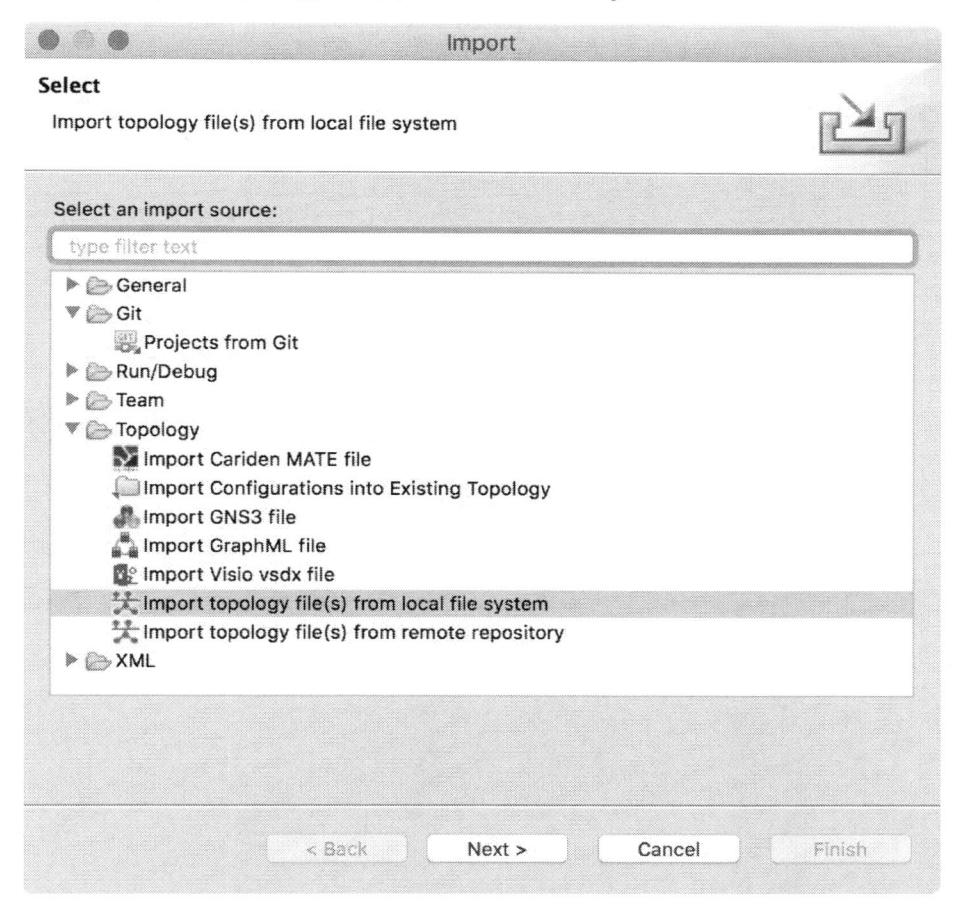

Browse to the folders where topology files are located. Select the topology folder. Make sure "create top-level folder" is checked for better folder organization. Click "Finish" and your topology files will be imported into VM Maestro client. Note that the imported files are located on your computer, not on the VIRL server.

For more in-depth explanations on how to use VM Maestro Client, working with VIRL files in a collaborative environment, utilizing Git Repository and more, refer to the The VIRL BOOK at:

www.virlbook.com

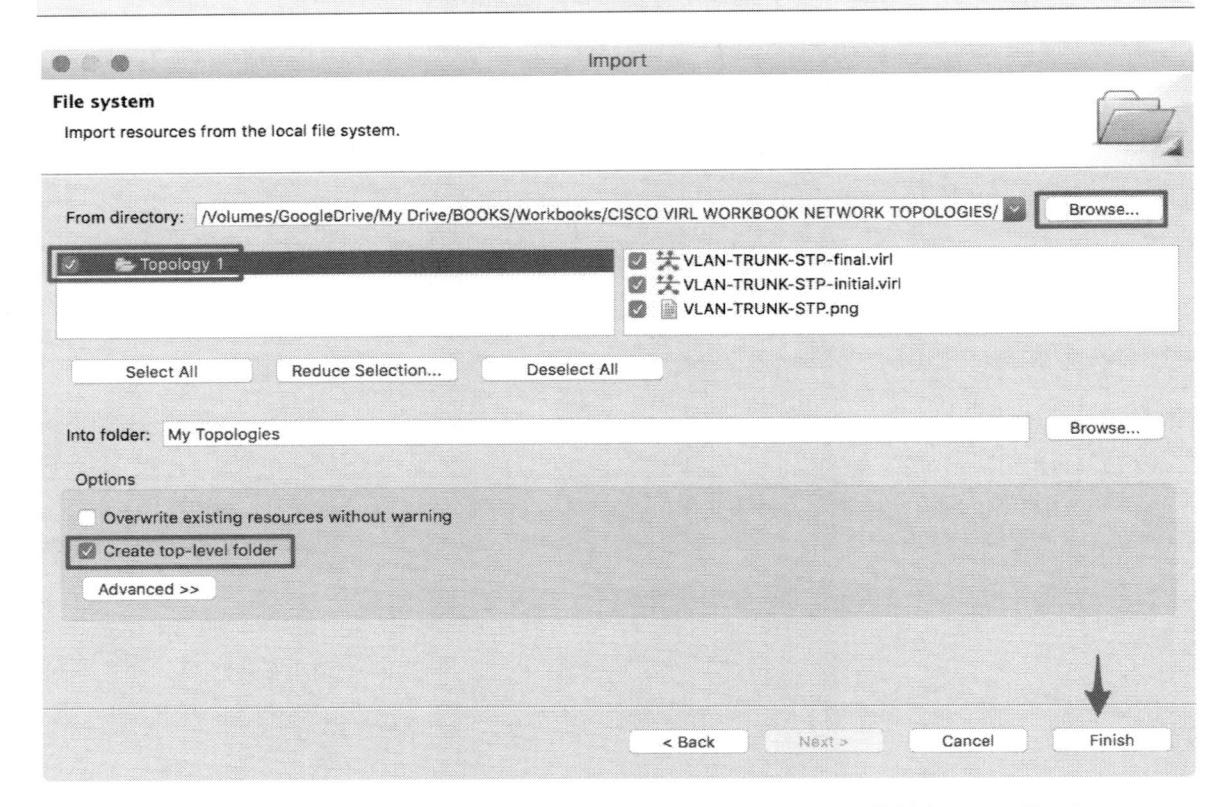

Double click on the "initial.virl" file to load the initial topology to VM Maestro Design window.

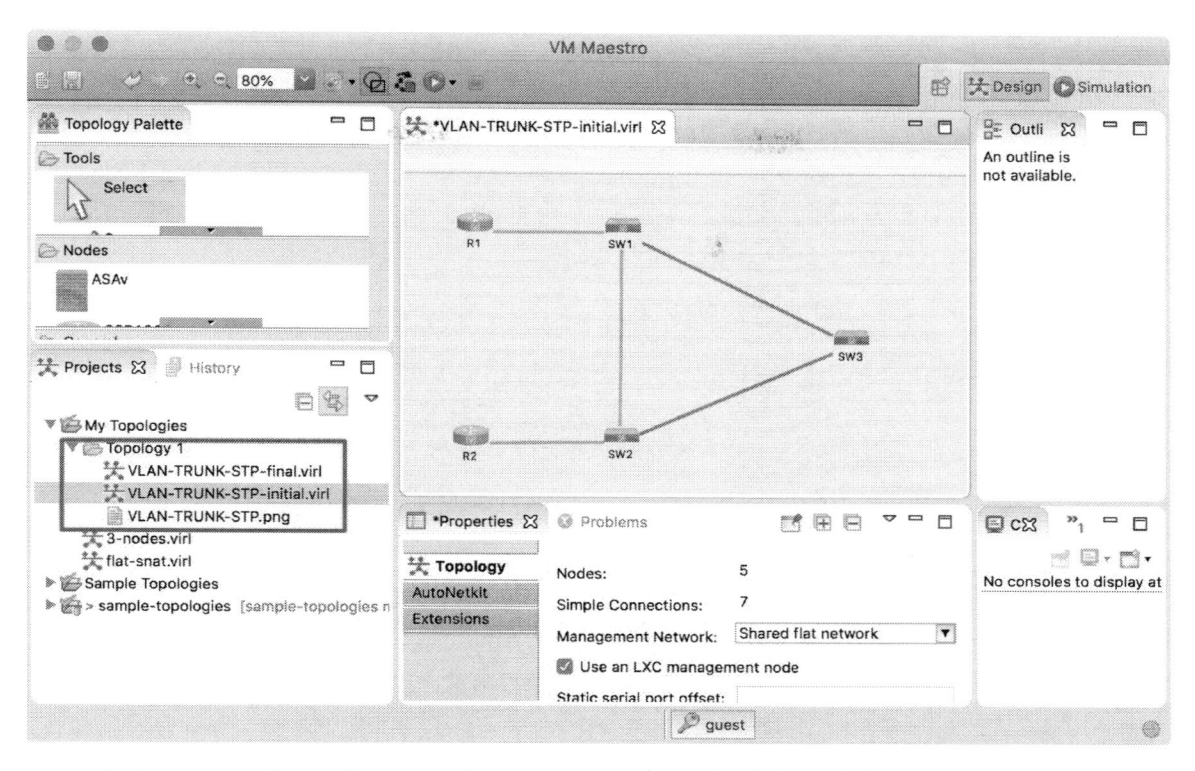

Launch the simulation without making any changes. Switch to "Simulation" view and wait till all the nodes are green and ACTIVE.

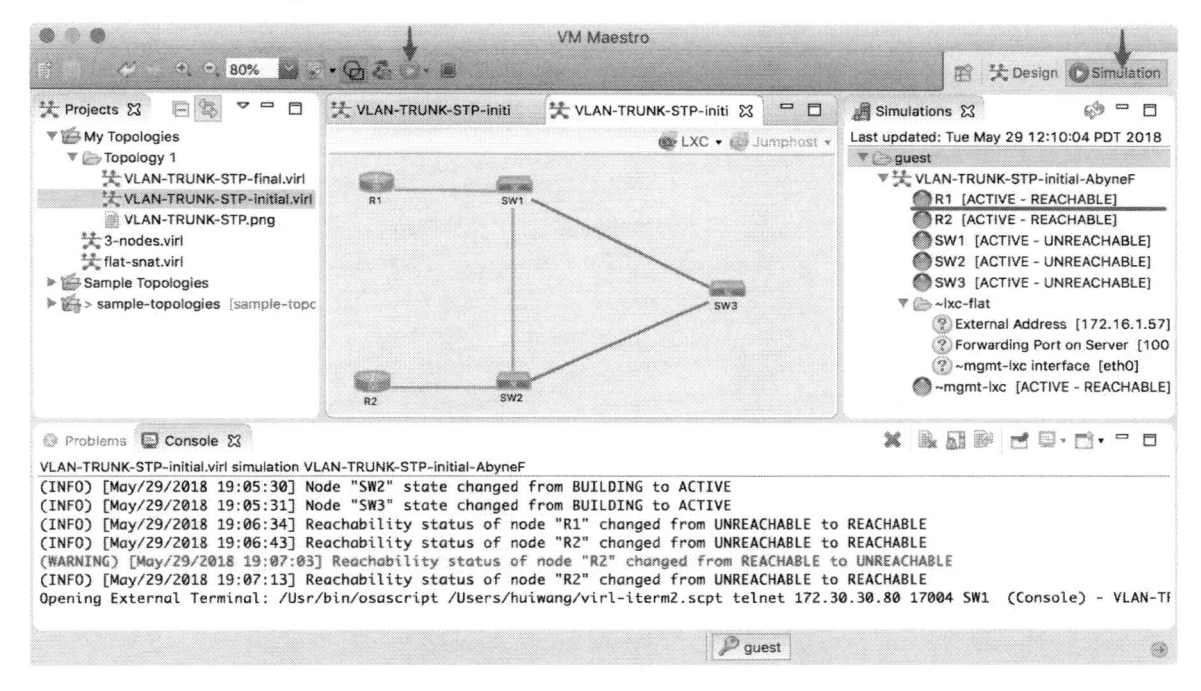

Opening CLI Console to Each Simulated Node

Depending on the number of nodes you are launching and your VIRL server's performance, it may take 3-5 minutes for all the nodes to boot up and routing tables to converge. Once all the nodes are up and running, you can access its CLI via Console Port. Right click on a node and select "Telnet > to its Console port". VM Maestro client will connect to the node and display the CLI window in the lower pane of VM Maestro client. Each additional CLI window you open, it'll be added as a tab. If you prefer using your own Telnet/SSH client such as Putty, Secure CRT or iTerm for Mac users, follow **Appendix A: Using External Telnet SSH Clients**.

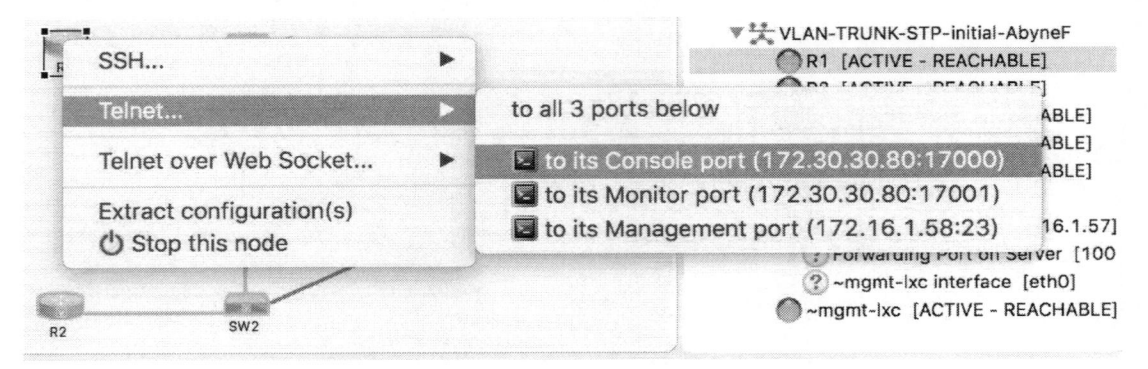

Gratulations! You have been prepared and you are ready to start your labs.

Topology 1: VLAN, Trunking, STP and Ether-Channel

Overview

This lab focuses on Layer-2 switching technologies on a LAN. Creating multiple VLANs and Trunking on the switches, designating root switch for Spanning-tree protocol, and build Link Aggregation Groups (LAG) among switches. This scenario is commonly seen in Cisco certification exams as well as real-world environment at the access-layer switches level. By completing this lab, you'll learn and set solid knowledge foundations on building a highly redundant, efficient and loop-free Layer-2 switching infrastructure.

Network Topology

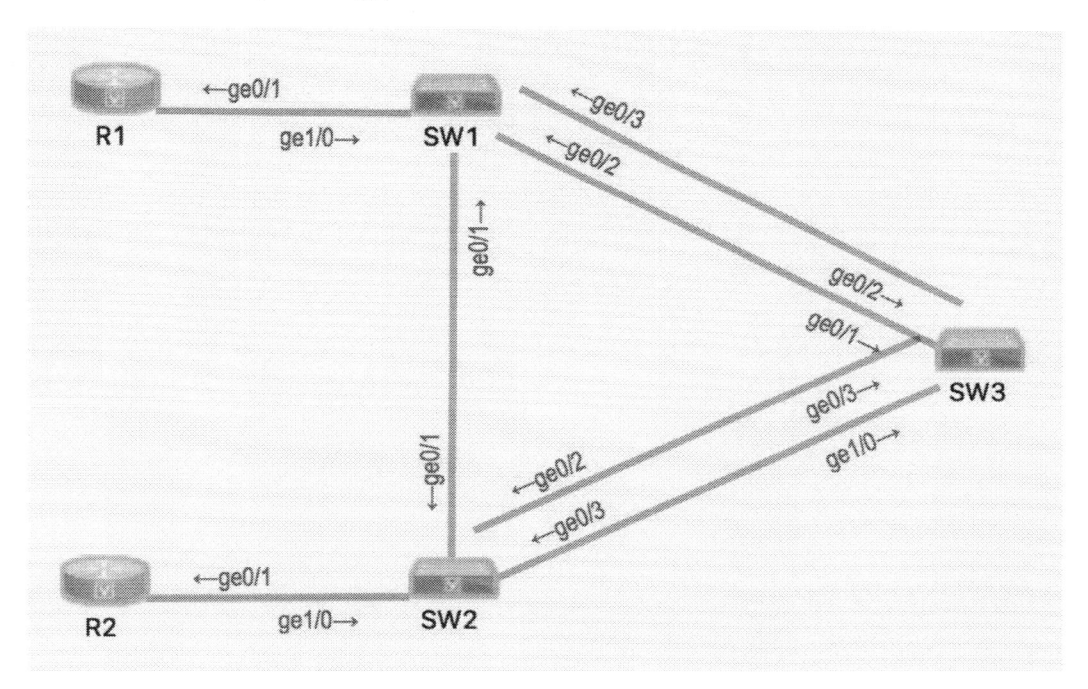

The network topology includes three switches and two routers. The routers are used to mimic end user's PC. They can be used to perform Ping and Traceroute testing.

What has been completed in the initial configuration:

- Wiring among the switches and routers
- Host names
- OOB management IP addresses
- Username / Password for switches and routers: cisco / cisco

Requirements

1. Configure VLAN Trunking on all inter-connected switch ports without using dynamic negotiation protocol. Only allow VLAN 10, 20 and 30 through the Trunk ports.

2. Create VLAN 10, 20 and 30 and shutdown VLAN 1 on all switches. Make SW3 VTP server and SW1 and SW2 VTP clients.

3. Configure Ether-channels on the dual-links between SW1-SW3 and SW2-SW3. Use non-cisco proprietary protocol for Link Aggregation Groups (LAG). Make SW3 start the grouping negotiations with SW1 and SW2.

4. Configure management IP on VLAN 10 on all the switches and enable Telnet access.

5. Configure host facing switch ports on VLAN 10 and apply best practice configuration so that the switch ports will go to forwarding state immediately.

6. Make SW3 the "root" switch for VLAN 10, 20 and 30.

7. Finally make sure you have a fully working network, with no errors or warnings in "show logging" and R1 can ping R2.

Solutions

1. Configure VLAN Trunking on all inter-connected switch ports without using dynamic negotiation protocol. Only allow VLAN 10, 20 and 30 through the Trunk ports

Double click on each node in the Simulation view. The nodes will expand to show which network ports are used to connect to each other.

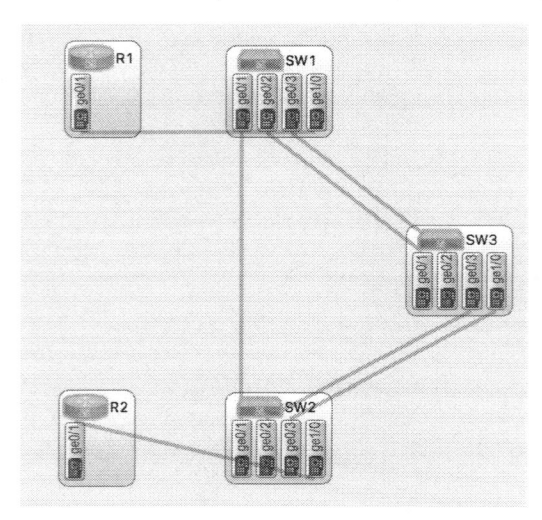

As observed from the interconnectivity map, SW1, and SW2 use Gig 0/1, 0/2 and 0/3 for inter-switch connections. SW3 uses all 4 ports. We shall configure these ports in Trunk mode.

On SW1 and SW2:

```
SW1,2#config t
Enter configuration commands, one per line.  End with CNTL/Z.
SW1,2(config)#interface range gig 0/1 - 3 ! define interface range
SW1,2(config-if-range)# switchport trunk allowed vlan 10-30 ! only allow vlan10-30 through truck ports
SW1,2(config-if-range)# switchport trunk encapsulation dot1q ! use dot1q as encapsulation protocol
SW1,2(config-if-range)# switchport mode trunk ! hard-code switchports in trunk mode
SW1,2(config-if-range)#^Z
SW1,2#

SW1#sho run int gig 0/1
Building configuration...
Current configuration : 217 bytes
!
interface GigabitEthernet0/1
 description to SW2
 switchport trunk allowed vlan 10-30
 switchport trunk encapsulation dot1q
 switchport mode trunk
 media-type rj45
 speed 1000
 duplex full
 no negotiation auto
end
```

On SW3:

```
SW3#config t
Enter configuration commands, one per line.  End with CNTL/Z.
SW3(config)#int range gig 0/1 - 3,gig1/0
SW3(config-if-range)# switchport trunk allowed vlan 10-30
SW3(config-if-range)# switchport trunk encapsulation dot1q
SW3(config-if-range)# switchport mode trunk
SW3(config-if-range)#^Z
SW3#
```

2. Configure VTP, make SW3 the VTP server and SW1 and SW2 the clients. Create VLAN 10, 20 and 30 and shutdown VLAN 1 on all switches

The idea behind VTP infrastructure is that you make a switch the VTP "server" and the rest of the switches as "client". All the VLAN management is done on the server. When you create, modify or delete VLANs on the VTP server, the information will be propagated to all the clients thus VLANs on the client switches are synchronized with the server switch. Why can't we just create these VLANs on individual switches? Let's say you have a fairly large network comprised of several dozens to a hundred switches. Do you want to touch every single switch to make a new VLAN? Secondly it is for consistency. You want to maintain a unified VLAN infrastructure on your entire network. VTP packets are exchanged via Trunk ports only. That's why we needed to configure port Trunking in Step 1.

Configure VTP domain (SNS), password (SNS) and make SW3 a server.

```
SW3#config t
Enter configuration commands, one per line.  End with CNTL/Z.
SW3(config)#vtp domain SNS
SW3(config)#vtp password SNS
SW3(config)#vtp mode server
```

Configure SW1 and SW2 and make them VTP clients. The domain and password must match.

```
SW1,2#config t
Enter configuration commands, one per line.  End with CNTL/Z.
SW1,2(config)#vtp domain SNS
SW1,2(config)#vtp password SNS
SW1,2(config)#vtp mode client
```

Verify VTP status on switches.

```
SW1,2,3#show vtp status
```

```
SW3#sho vtp status
VTP Version capable             : 1 to 3
VTP version running             : 1
VTP Domain Name                 : SNS
VTP Pruning Mode                : Disabled
VTP Traps Generation            : Disabled
Device ID                       : 5e00.0002.8000
Configuration last modified by 172.16.1.189 at 8-25-18 18:05:12
Local updater ID is 172.16.1.189 on interface Gi0/0 (first layer3 interface foun
d)

Feature VLAN:
----------------
VTP Operating Mode              : Server
Maximum VLANs supported locally : 1005
Number of existing VLANs        : 9
Configuration Revision          : 1
MD5 digest                      : 0xB3 0xD2 0x57 0xA1 0x2F 0x2F 0x14 0x76
                                  0xAC 0xDD 0x4C 0x7C 0xA0 0x11 0xFA 0x18
```

```
SW1#sho vtp status
VTP Version capable             : 1 to 3
VTP version running             : 1
VTP Domain Name                 : SNS
VTP Pruning Mode                : Disabled
VTP Traps Generation            : Disabled
Device ID                       : 5e00.0000.8000
Configuration last modified by 172.16.1.189 at 8-25-18 18:05:12

Feature VLAN:
----------------
VTP Operating Mode              : Client
Maximum VLANs supported locally : 1005
Number of existing VLANs        : 9
Configuration Revision          : 1
MD5 digest                      : 0xB3 0xD2 0x57 0xA1 0x2F 0x2F 0x14 0x76
                                  0xAC 0xDD 0x4C 0x7C 0xA0 0x11 0xFA 0x18
```

Review the existing VLANs on the switches. Configure VLAN 10, 20 and 30 on SW3 only.

```
SW1>enable
Password:cisco
SW1# show vlan brief
```

```
SW1# show vlan brief

VLAN Name                          Status    Ports
---- ------------------------------ --------- -------
1    default                        active
2    ank_vlan2                      active    Gi1/0
1002 fddi-default                   act/unsup
1003 token-ring-default             act/unsup
1004 fddinet-default                act/unsup
1005 trnet-default                  act/unsup
```

The exiting VLANs are VLAN 1, 2 and 1002-1005. Create new VLAN 10, 20 and 30 on SW3 only. Shutdown VLAN 1 on all switches.

```
SW3#config t
Enter configuration commands, one per line.  End with CNTL/Z.
SW3(config)#vlan 10,20,30
SW1(config-vlan)#exit

SW1,2,3(config)#interface vlan 1
SW1,2,3(config-if)#shutdown
SW1,2,3(config)#^Z
```

Log in each switch and exam the new VLANs. SW1 and SW2 should have learned the new VLANs from SW3. Verify VLAN 1 interface has been shut down.

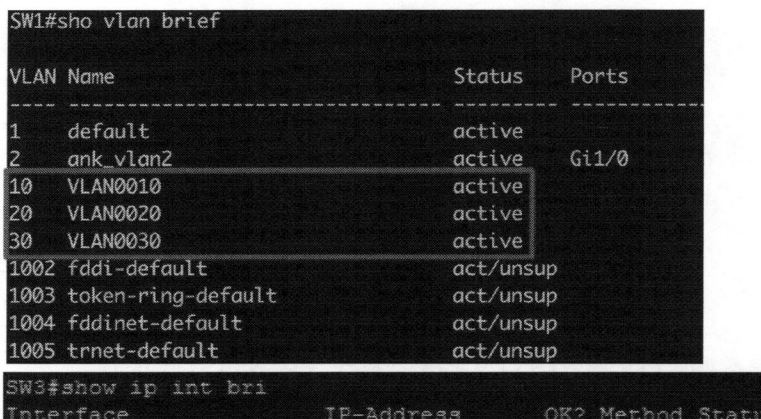

```
SW1#sho vlan brief

VLAN Name                             Status    Ports
---- -------------------------------- --------- -------------------------------
1    default                          active
2    ank_vlan2                        active    Gi1/0
10   VLAN0010                         active
20   VLAN0020                         active
30   VLAN0030                         active
1002 fddi-default                     act/unsup
1003 token-ring-default               act/unsup
1004 fddinet-default                  act/unsup
1005 trnet-default                    act/unsup
```

```
SW3#show ip int bri
Interface              IP-Address      OK? Method Status                Protocol
GigabitEthernet0/0     172.16.1.189    YES NVRAM  administratively down down
GigabitEthernet0/1     unassigned      YES unset  up                    up
GigabitEthernet0/2     unassigned      YES unset  administratively down down
GigabitEthernet0/3     unassigned      YES unset  administratively down down
GigabitEthernet1/0     unassigned      YES unset  up                    up
Loopback0              unassigned      YES unset  up                    up
Vlan1                  unassigned      YES unset  administratively down down
```

3. **Configure Ether-channels on the dual-links between SW1-SW3 and SW2-SW3. Use non-cisco proprietary protocol for Link Aggregation Groups (LAG). Make SW3 start the grouping negotiations with SW1 and SW2**

Starting with SW1, configure a Port-Channel that will be used for connecting to SW3. The port-channel configuration must carry the same trunk configuration that the individual interfaces have. Finally, we tell interface Gig 0/2 and Gig 0/3 to use Port-channel 1. Think of Port-channel is a logical bundle, which represents multiple physical interfaces inside. Therefore, all the interface configuration must match.

```
SW1#config t
Enter configuration commands, one per line.  End with CNTL/Z.
SW1(config)#interface Port-channel1 ! configure Port-channel 1
```

```
SW1(config-if)# switchport trunk allowed vlan 10-30
SW1(config-if)# switchport trunk encapsulation dot1q
SW1(config-if)# switchport mode trunk
SW1(config-if)#exit

SW1(config)#interface range gig 0/2-3 ! define interface range
SW1(config-if-range)# channel-group 1 mode passive ! configure LACP
passive mode
SW1(config-if-range)#

*May 29 21:00:07.326: %LINEPROTO-5-UPDOWN: Line protocol on Interface
GigabitEthernet0/2, changed state to down

*May 29 21:00:07.338: %LINEPROTO-5-UPDOWN: Line protocol on Interface
GigabitEthernet0/3, changed state to down

*May 29 21:00:13.770: %SYS-5-CONFIG_I: Configured from console by
console

*May 29 21:00:14.342: %EC-5-L3DONTBNDL2: Gi0/2 suspended: LACP
currently not enabled on the remote port.

*May 29 21:00:14.410: %EC-5-L3DONTBNDL2: Gi0/3 suspended: LACP
currently not enabled on the remote port.
```

Repeat the same configuration on SW2. On SW3, we will create two Port-channels. One for the connection to SW1 and the other for the connection to SW2. We assign Gig 0/1, 0/2 to Port-channel 1 and Gig 0/3, 1/0 to Port-channel 2. Finally, we make SW3 actively negotiate link aggregation with SW1 and SW2.

```
SW3#config t
Enter configuration commands, one per line.  End with CNTL/Z.
SW3(config)#interface Port-channel1
SW3(config-if)# switchport trunk allowed vlan 10-30
SW3(config-if)# switchport trunk encapsulation dot1q
SW3(config-if)# switchport mode trunk
SW3(config-if)#exit

SW3(config-if)#interface Port-channel2
SW3(config-if)# switchport trunk allowed vlan 10-30
SW3(config-if)# switchport trunk encapsulation dot1q
SW3(config-if)# switchport mode trunk
SW3(config-if)#exit

SW3(config)#interface range gig 0/1-2
SW3(config-if-range)#channel-group 1 mode active
SW3(config-if-range)#exit
*Jun  3 16:18:34.849: %LINK-3-UPDOWN: Interface Port-channel1, changed
```

```
state to up
*Jun  3 16:18:35.851: %LINEPROTO-5-UPDOWN: Line protocol on Interface
Port-channel1, changed state to up

SW3(config)#interface range gig 0/3,gig1/0
SW3(config-if-range)#channel-group 2 mode active
SW3(config-if-range)#exit
SW3#

*Jun  3 16:19:03.694: %LINK-3-UPDOWN: Interface Port-channel2, changed
state to up
*Jun  3 16:19:04.693: %LINEPROTO-5-UPDOWN: Line protocol on Interface
Port-channel2, changed state to up
```

Verify the Ether-channels have been built correctly. It appears that Gig0/2 and Gig0/3 on SW3 are showing "D", which means "Down".

```
SW3#sho etherchannel summary
```

```
SW3#sho etherchannel summary
Flags:  D - down        P - bundled in port-channel
        I - stand-alone s - suspended
        H - Hot-standby (LACP only)
        R - Layer3      S - Layer2
        U - in use      N - not in use, no aggregation
        f - failed to allocate aggregator

        M - not in use, minimum links not met
        m - not in use, port not aggregated due to minimum links not met
        u - unsuitable for bundling
        w - waiting to be aggregated
        d - default port

        A - formed by Auto LAG


Number of channel-groups in use: 2
Number of aggregators:           2

Group  Port-channel  Protocol    Ports
------+-------------+-----------+-----------------------------------------------
1      Po1(SU)         LACP      Gi0/1(P)    Gi0/2(D)
2      Po2(SU)         LACP      Gi0/3(D)    Gi1/0(P)
```

Review the port status on SW3. Looks like port Gig0/2 and Gig0/3 are administratively "disabled".

```
SW3#show interface status
SW3(config)#interface range gig 0/2-3
SW3(config)#no shutdown
```

```
SW3#show interfaces status

Port    Name              Status      Vlan     Duplex   Speed  Type
Gi0/0   OOB management    disabled    routed   auto     auto   RJ45
Gi0/1   to SW1            connected   trunk    full     1000   RJ45
Gi0/2   to SW1            disabled    1        auto     auto   RJ45
Gi0/3   to SW2            disabled    1        auto     auto   RJ45
Gi1/0   to SW2            connected   trunk    full     1000   RJ45
Po1                       connected   trunk    a-full   1000
Po2                       connected   trunk    a-full   1000

*Jun  3 16:30:52.964: %LINK-3-UPDOWN: Interface GigabitEthernet0/2, changed state to up
*Jun  3 16:30:53.181: %LINK-3-UPDOWN: Interface GigabitEthernet0/3, changed state to up
SW3#
*Jun  3 16:30:53.582: %SYS-5-CONFIG_I: Configured from console by console
*Jun  3 16:30:54.172: %EC-5-CANNOT_BUNDLE2: Gi0/2 is not compatible with Gi0/1 and will be suspended (speed of Gi0/2 is auto
, Gi0/1 is 1000M)
*Jun  3 16:30:54.384: %EC-5-CANNOT_BUNDLE2: Gi0/3 is not compatible with Gi1/0 and will be suspended (speed of Gi0/3 is auto
, Gi1/0 is 1000M)
```

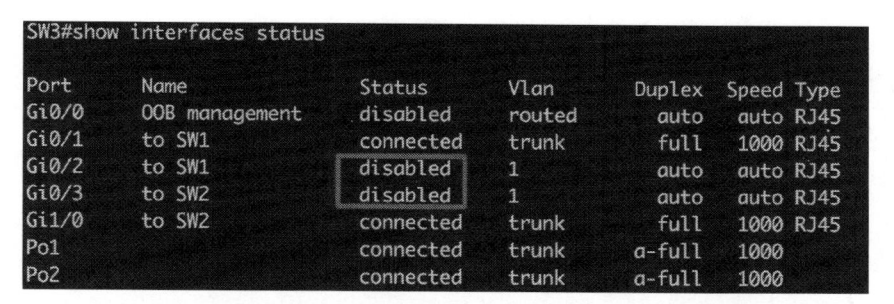

Here we got another problem. Interface bundling requires all the interfaces being bundled have exactly same physical types and logical configuration. The error messages indicate that Gig0/2 and Gig0/1 have different speed configuration, one is configured "auto" and the other is configured "1000M". We can address this issue by configuring all the interfaces on SW3 being used for Ether-channels "auto" speed and "full duplex".

```
SW3#config t
Enter configuration commands, one per line.  End with CNTL/Z.
SW3(config)#int range gig 0/1-3,gig1/0
SW3(config-if-range)#dup
SW3(config-if-range)#duplex full
SW3(config-if-range)#speed auto
SW3(config-if-range)#
*Jun  3 16:39:49.517: %LINEPROTO-5-UPDOWN: Line protocol on Interface GigabitEthernet0/2, changed state to up
*Jun  3 16:39:49.743: %LINEPROTO-5-UPDOWN: Line protocol on Interface GigabitEthernet0/3, changed state to up
*Jun  3 16:39:55.798: %EC-5-COMPATIBLE: Gi0/2 is compatible with port-channel members
*Jun  3 16:39:55.822: %EC-5-COMPATIBLE: Gi0/3 is compatible with port-channel members
*Jun  3 16:39:57.821: %LINK-3-UPDOWN: Interface Port-channel2, changed state to down
*Jun  3 16:39:58.821: %LINEPROTO-5-UPDOWN: Line protocol on Interface Port-channel2, changed state to down
*Jun  3 16:40:03.456: %LINK-3-UPDOWN: Interface Port-channel2, changed state to up
*Jun  3 16:40:04.455: %LINEPROTO-5-UPDOWN: Line protocol on Interface Port-channel2, changed state to up
```

Validate the Ether-channels on SW3. Make sure all interfaces within each Ether-channel Group shows "P - bundled in port-channel".

```
SW3#show etherchannel summary
```

```
Number of channel-groups in use: 2
Number of aggregators:           2

Group  Port-channel  Protocol    Ports
------+-------------+-----------+-----------------------------------------------
1      Po1(SU)         LACP      Gi0/1(P)    Gi0/2(P)
2      Po2(SU)         LACP      Gi0/3(P)    Gi1/0(P)
```

The requirements have been configured and you can move on to the next task.

If you want to learn more about Link Aggregation protocols and how they can be configured on Cisco switches, here is a quick summary.

EtherChannel bundles individual Ethernet links into a single logical link that provides additional bandwidth and link redundancy between two Cisco Catalyst switches. All interfaces in each EtherChannel must be the same speed and duplex, and both ends of the channel must be configured as either a Layer 2 or Layer 3 interface. In case a link within the EtherChannel bundle fails, traffic previously carried over the failed link is carried over the remaining links within the EtherChannel. There are two protocols used for the link aggregation:

- Cisco's proprietary Port Aggregation Protocol (PAgP).
- IEEE standard Link Aggregation Protocol (LACP)

PAgP modes configuration

Mode (PAgP)	Description
Auto	Places an interface into a passive negotiating state, in which the interface responds to PAgP packets it receives but does not start PAgP packet negotiation. This setting minimizes the transmission of PAgP packets and is the default.
Desirable	Places an interface into an active negotiating state, in which the interface starts negotiations with other interfaces by sending PAgP packets.
On	Forces the interface to channel without negotiation. With the on mode, a usable EtherChannel exists only when an interface group in the on mode is connected to another interface group in the on mode. Neither PAgP nor LACP is involved.

LACP modes configuration

Mode (LACP)	Description
Passive	The switch does not initiate the channel but does understand incoming LACP packets. The peer (in active state) initiates negotiation (by sending out an LACP packet) which we receive and reply to, eventually forming the aggregation channel with the peer. This is similar to the auto mode in PAgP.

Active	We are willing to form an aggregate link and initiate the negotiation. The link aggregate will be formed if the other end is running in LACP active or passive mode. This is similar to the desirable mode of PAgP.
On	Forces the interface to channel without negotiation. With the on mode, a usable EtherChannel exists only when an interface group in the on mode is connected to another interface group in the on mode. Neither PAgP nor LACP is involved.

4. Configure management IP on VLAN 10 on all the switches and enable Telnet access

Log in each switch and configure a management IP address for VLAN10. We follow certain IP addressing scheme to make the IP addresses easy to remember. Refer to **Appendix B: Node Naming and IP Addressing Scheme**.

```
SW1(config)#interface Vlan10
SW1(config-if)# ip address 22.1.12.21 255.255.255.0
SW1(config-if)#no shutdown

SW2(config)#interface Vlan10
SW2(config-if)# ip address 22.1.12.22 255.255.255.0
SW2(config-if)#no shutdown

SW3(config)#interface Vlan10
SW3(config-if)# ip address 22.1.12.23 255.255.255.0
SW3(config-if)#no shutdown
```

Configure Telnet access on all switches.

```
SW1,SW2(config)#line vty 0 4
SW1,SW2(config)# exec-timeout 0 0
SW1,SW2(config)# password cisco
SW1,SW2(config)# login
SW1,SW2(config)# transport input telnet ssh
SW1,SW2#
```

5. Configure host facing switch ports on VLAN 10 and apply best practice configuration so that the switch ports will go to forwarding state immediately

According to the physical wiring diagram, both SW1 and SW2 use Gig1/0 to connect to a host, in this case R1 and R2. Under the interface configuration mode, configuring spanning-tree PortFast mode. PortFast causes a switch or trunk port to enter the spanning tree forwarding state immediately, bypassing the listening and learning states. You can use PortFast on switch ports that are connected to a single workstation, switch, or server to allow those devices to connect to the network immediately, instead of waiting for the port to transition from the listening and learning states to the forwarding state.

Note that you should only configure PortFast on a switch port to connect to a single host. If you enable PortFast on a port that is connected to another Layer 2 device, such as a switch, you might create network loops.

```
SW1,SW2(config)#interface gig1/0
SW1,SW2(config)#switchport access vlan 10
SW1,SW2(config-if)#speed auto
SW1,SW2(config-if)#duplex full
SW1,SW2(config-if)#spanning-tree portfast edge
```

```
interface GigabitEthernet1/0
 description to R1
 switchport access vlan 10
 switchport mode access
 media-type rj45
 duplex full
 no negotiation auto
 spanning-tree portfast edge
end
```

6. Make SW3 the "root" switch for VLAN 10, 20 and 30

STP (Spanning-tree Protocol) root bridge election is based on the priority and MAC address fields of the Bridge ID. The device with the lowest priority value is elected the root. If there is a tie in priority, the device with the lowest MAC address is elected root.

First, we take a look who is the "root" switch for VLAN 10. Exam the output of "show spanning-tree vlan 10" on SW3 and SW1, the "root" switch for VLAN 10 is SW1.

```
SW1#show spanning-tree vlan 10
```

```
SW3#sho spanning-tree vlan 10

VLAN0010
  Spanning tree enabled protocol ieee
  Root ID    Priority    32778
             Address     5e00.0000.0000
             Cost        3
             Port        65 (Port-channel1)
             Hello Time  2 sec  Max Age 20 sec  Forward Delay 15 sec

  Bridge ID  Priority    32778  (priority 32768 sys-id-ext 10)
             Address     5e00.0002.0000
             Hello Time  2 sec  Max Age 20 sec  Forward Delay 15 sec
             Aging Time  300 sec

Interface           Role Sts Cost      Prio.Nbr Type
------------------- ---- --- --------- -------- --------------------------------
Po1                 Root FWD 3         128.65   P2p
Po2                 Desg FWD 3         128.66   P2p
```

```
SW1#sho spanning-tree vlan 10

VLAN0010
  Spanning tree enabled protocol ieee
  Root ID    Priority    32778
             Address     5e00.0000.0000
             This bridge is the root
             Hello Time  2 sec  Max Age 20 sec  Forward Delay 15 sec

  Bridge ID  Priority    32778  (priority 32768 sys-id-ext 10)
             Address     5e00.0000.0000
             Hello Time  2 sec  Max Age 20 sec  Forward Delay 15 sec
             Aging Time  300 sec

Interface           Role Sts Cost      Prio.Nbr Type
------------------- ---- --- --------- -------- --------------------------------
Gi0/1               Desg FWD 4         128.2    P2p
Po1                 Desg FWD 3         128.65   P2p
```

"root" switch for other VLANs can be verified with the same command. You'll find that SW1 is the "root" switch for all VLAN 10, 20 and 30.

To make SW3 the "root" switch for VLAN 10, 20 and 30, configure its priority of zero. On SW3, issue this command:

```
SW3(config)#spanning-tree vlan 10,20,30 priority 0
```

SW3 shows that **This bridge is the root**. The root bridge should show the same priority and MAC address for both the Root ID and the Bridge ID and list all interfaces as Designated ports (downstream facing). In this case, SW3's BID is **5e00.0002.0000**.

```
SW3#show spa
SW3#show spanning-tree vlan 10

VLAN0010
  Spanning tree enabled protocol ieee
  Root ID    Priority    10
             Address     5e00.0002.0000
             This bridge is the root
             Hello Time  2 sec  Max Age 20 sec  Forward Delay 15 sec

  Bridge ID  Priority    10    (priority 0 sys-id-ext 10)
             Address     5e00.0002.0000
             Hello Time  2 sec  Max Age 20 sec  Forward Delay 15 sec
             Aging Time  300 sec

Interface           Role Sts Cost      Prio.Nbr Type
------------------- ---- --- --------- -------- --------------------------------
Po1                 Desg FWD 3         128.65   P2p
Po2                 Desg FWD 3         128.66   P2p
```

Verify Spanning-tree root for VLAN 20 and 30. SW3 is now the "root" switch for all.

7. Finally make sure you have a fully working network, with no errors or warnings in "show logging" and R1 can ping R2

Log in each switch and confirm there is no reoccurring errors or warnings in the logs.

```
SW1,SW2,SW3#Show logging
```

Log in R1 and R2, exam the IP addresses configured on the interface connected to SW1 and SW2 respectively. (IP addresses have been pre-configured in the initial configuration file) On R1, make sure you can ping R2 at 22.1.12.2. And on R2, make sure you can ping R1 at 22.1.12.1.

```
R1#show ip int brief
Interface              IP-Address      OK? Method Status    Protocol
GigabitEthernet0/0     172.16.1.53     YES NVRAM  up        up
GigabitEthernet0/1     22.1.12.1       YES NVRAM  up        up
Loopback0              1.1.1.1         YES NVRAM  up        up
R1#
R1#ping 22.1.12.2
Type escape sequence to abort.
Sending 5, 100-byte ICMP Echos to 22.1.12.2, timeout is 2 seconds:
!!!!!
Success rate is 100 percent (5/5), round-trip min/avg/max = 11/14/17 ms
R1#
```

```
R2#show ip int brief
Interface              IP-Address      OK? Method Status                Protocol
GigabitEthernet0/0     172.16.1.54     YES NVRAM  up                    up
GigabitEthernet0/1     22.1.12.2       YES NVRAM  up                    up
Loopback0              2.2.2.2         YES NVRAM  up                    up
R2#
R2#ping 22.1.12.1
Type escape sequence to abort.
Sending 5, 100-byte ICMP Echos to 22.1.12.1, timeout is 2 seconds:
!!!!!
Success rate is 100 percent (5/5), round-trip min/avg/max = 15/18/22 ms
R2#
```

You can also use "show cdp neighbors" command to display directly connected peers with Cisco Discovery Protocol enabled. The initial configuration has CDP enabled on all nodes.

```
SW1#show cdp neighbors
```

```
SW1#show cdp neighbors
Capability Codes: R - Router, T - Trans Bridge, B - Source Route Bridge
                  S - Switch, H - Host, I - IGMP, r - Repeater, P - Phone,
                  D - Remote, C - CVTA, M - Two-port Mac Relay

Device ID       Local Intrfce    Holdtme    Capability  Platform  Port ID
SW2             Gig 0/1          165          R S I               Gig 0/1
SW3             Gig 0/3          140          R S I               Gig 0/2
SW3             Gig 0/2          130          R S I               Gig 0/1
R1.virl.info    Gig 1/0          141          R B                 Gig 0/1

Total cdp entries displayed : 4
```

To verify CDP is enabled, go to VM Maestro client's Design view and confirm "Enable CDP" is set to "True" under AutoNetkit general settings.

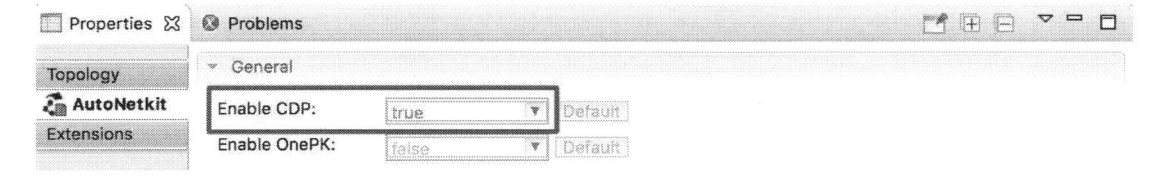

Congratulations, you have completed all tasks in Topology 1.

Topology 2: Configuring EIGRP IPv4 and IPv6

Overview

Enhanced Interior Gateway Routing Protocol (EIGRP) is an advanced distance vector routing protocol based on the principles of the Interior Gateway Routing Protocol (IGRP). EIGRP is developed by Cisco and operate only on their devices. EIGRP uses bandwidth, delay, load and reliability to calculate the metric for its routing table (not hop count used by legacy protocols). For this reason, EIGRP always selects and calculates the most optimal route for efficiency. EIGRP uses a DUAL algorithm to avoid loops and send occasional hello packets to check the status of neighbor routers.

In this lab, we'll configure a fully converged network by utilizing EIGRP protocol. Same exercise will be implemented using IPv6.

Network Topology

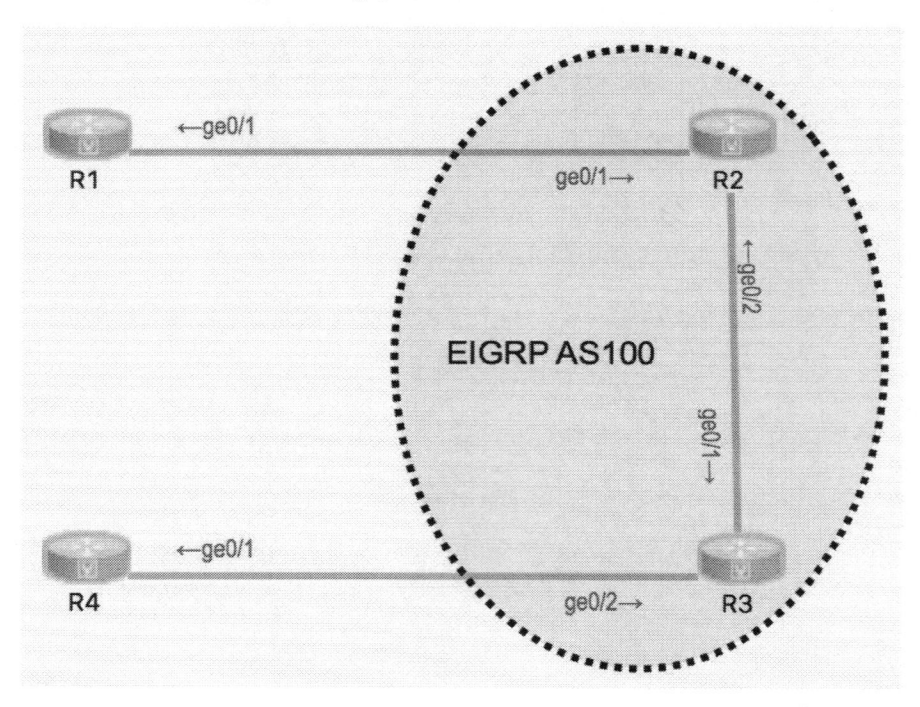

The network topology includes four routers. Only R2 and R3 participate in EIGRP routing. R1 and R4 are used to mimic end user's PC. They do not participate in dynamic routing and can be used to perform Ping and Traceroute testing.

What has been done in the initial configuration:

- Wiring among the switches and routers
- Host names
- OOB management IP addresses and loopback0 address
- Username / Password for switches and routers: cisco / cisco

Requirements

1. Configure EIGRP using autonomous number 100 between R2 and R3.

2. R2 and R3 shall advertise their directly connected interface subnets as well as their Loopback0 addresses to EIGRP neighbors.

3. "auto summary" shall be disabled.

4. R1 and R4 shall use their directly connected upstream router as their default gateway. Configure a static route on them.

5. Finally make sure you have a fully working network, with no errors or warnings in "show logging". R1 can ping R4's Gig0/1 interface IP address, and so can R4 ping R1's Gig0/1 IP address.

6. Configure EIGRP for IPv6. Accomplish the same requirements as IPv4 outlined above.

Solutions

1. Configure EIGRP using autonomous number 100 between R2 and R3.

Double click on the nodes to expand and show their physical layer connections. You can also use "show cdp neighbor" do find out how the routers are interconnected together.

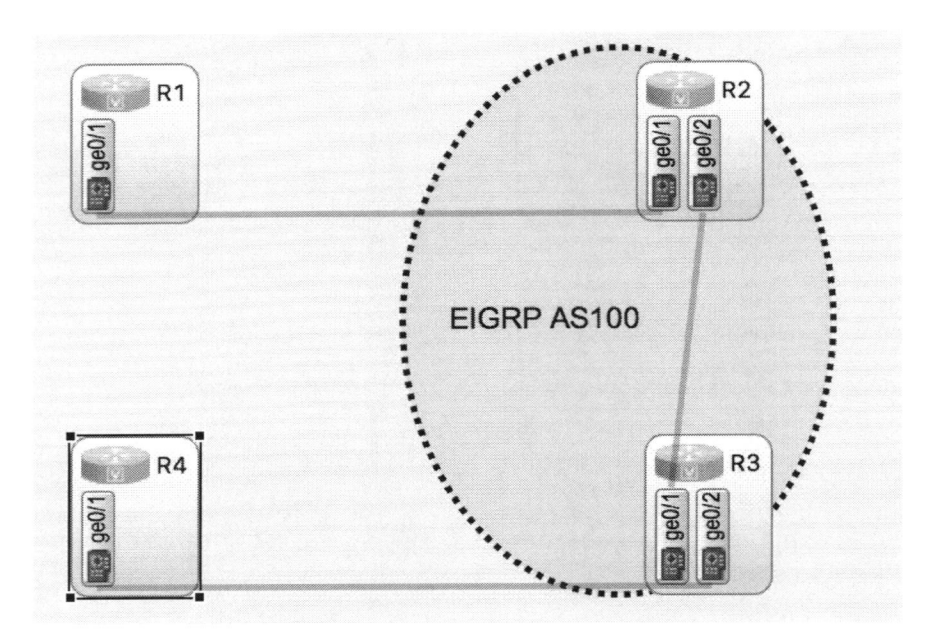

[Network diagram showing R1, R2, R3, R4 routers with EIGRP AS100]

Make sure the routers can ping their directly connected neighbors. Here is an example on R1.

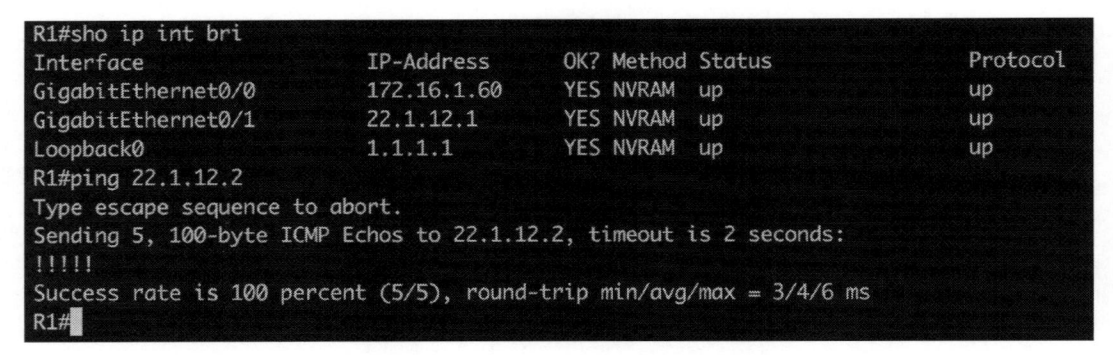

```
R1#sho ip int bri
Interface              IP-Address      OK? Method Status    Protocol
GigabitEthernet0/0     172.16.1.60     YES NVRAM  up        up
GigabitEthernet0/1     22.1.12.1       YES NVRAM  up        up
Loopback0              1.1.1.1         YES NVRAM  up        up
R1#ping 22.1.12.2
Type escape sequence to abort.
Sending 5, 100-byte ICMP Echos to 22.1.12.2, timeout is 2 seconds:
!!!!!
Success rate is 100 percent (5/5), round-trip min/avg/max = 3/4/6 ms
R1#
```

Enable EIGRP routing protocol on R2 and R3 with autonomous 100. Per requirements, we added the loopback and directedly connected interface IPs to participate in EIGRP.

R2#
```
R2(config)#router eigrp 100
R2(config-router)# network 2.2.2.2 0.0.0.0
R2(config-router)# network 22.1.0.0 0.0.255.255
R2#
```

R3#
```
R3(config)#router eigrp 100
R3(config-router)# network 3.3.3.3 0.0.0.0
R3(config-router)# network 22.1.0.0 0.0.255.255
R2#
```

2. **R2 and R3 shall advertise their directly connected interface subnets as well as their Loopback0 addresses to EIGRP neighbors.**

   This requirement has been completed in the previous step. Validate that EIGRP neighbor is up and the routing table has been populated.

```
R2#sho ip eigrp neighbors
```

```
R2#sho ip eigrp neighbors
EIGRP-IPv4 Neighbors for AS(100)
H   Address                 Interface           Hold Uptime   SRTT   RTO  Q  Seq
                                                (sec)         (ms)        Cnt Num
0   22.1.23.3               Gi0/2                12 00:03:03    8    100  0  3
R2#
```

```
R2#show ip route eigrp
```

```
R2#show ip route eigrp
Codes: L - local, C - connected, S - static, R - RIP, M - mobile, B - BGP
       D - EIGRP, EX - EIGRP external, O - OSPF, IA - OSPF inter area
       N1 - OSPF NSSA external type 1, N2 - OSPF NSSA external type 2
       E1 - OSPF external type 1, E2 - OSPF external type 2
       i - IS-IS, su - IS-IS summary, L1 - IS-IS level-1, L2 - IS-IS level-2
       ia - IS-IS inter area, * - candidate default, U - per-user static route
       o - ODR, P - periodic downloaded static route, H - NHRP, l - LISP
       a - application route
       + - replicated route, % - next hop override, p - overrides from PfR

Gateway of last resort is not set

      3.0.0.0/32 is subnetted, 1 subnets
D        3.3.3.3 [90/130816] via 22.1.23.3, 00:04:44, GigabitEthernet0/2
      22.0.0.0/8 is variably subnetted, 5 subnets, 2 masks
D        22.1.34.0/24 [90/3072] via 22.1.23.3, 00:04:44, GigabitEthernet0/2
R2#
```

We have verified that EIGRP routing has been configured correctly. Remote router's loopback routes and directly connected routes have been populated into the EIGRP routing tables.

3. **"auto summary" shall be disabled.**

   Auto summarization is a feature which allows EIGRP to summarize its routes to their classful networks automatically. For example, consider we are planning to use eight subnets of class B network 172.16.0.0/16. With "auto summary" turned on, only one super-net 172.16.0.0/16 will be injected into the routing table. It greatly reduces the size of the routing table and improves convergence speed shall any network changes occur.

- 172.16.0.0/19
- 172.16.32.0/19
- 172.16.64.0/19
- 172.16.96.0/19
- 172.16.128.0/19
- 172.16.160.0/19
- 172.16.192.0/19
- 172.16.224.0/19

By default, "auto-summary" is enabled. In our lab, we wanted to see the granularity of every subnets in the routing table for learning purpose. That's why we disable "auto-summary".

```
R2,R3(config)#router eigrp 100
R2,R3(config-router)#no auto-summary
```

To verify "auto-summary" has been disabled, use this command:

```
R2,R3#show ip protocols
```

```
Routing Protocol is "eigrp 100"
  Outgoing update filter list for all interfaces is not set
  Incoming update filter list for all interfaces is not set
  Default networks flagged in outgoing updates
  Default networks accepted from incoming updates
  EIGRP-IPv4 Protocol for AS(100)
    Metric weight K1=1, K2=0, K3=1, K4=0, K5=0
    Soft SIA disabled
    NSF-aware route hold timer is 240
    Router-ID: 2.2.2.2
    Topology : 0 (base)
      Active Timer: 3 min
      Distance: internal 90 external 170
      Maximum path: 4
      Maximum hopcount 100
      Maximum metric variance 1

  Automatic Summarization: disabled
  Maximum path: 4
  Routing for Networks:
    2.2.2.2/32
    22.1.0.0/16
  Routing Information Sources:
    Gateway         Distance      Last Update
    22.1.23.3            90        00:17:03
  Distance: internal 90 external 170
```

As you can see, using EIGRP, a router keeps a copy of its neighbor's routing tables. If it can't find a route to a destination in one of these tables, it queries its neighbors for a route and they in turn query their neighbors until a route is found. When a routing table entry changes in one of the routers, it notifies its neighbors of the change only (some earlier protocols require sending the entire table). To keep all routers aware of the state of neighbors, each router sends out a periodic "hello" packet. A router from which no "hello" packet has been received in a certain period of time is assumed to be inoperative. It's neighbors remove the inoperative router from their OSPF database and let the active neighbors know about the change.

4. **R1 and R4 shall use their directly connected upstream router as their default gateway. Configure a static route on them.**

   Consider we use R1 and R4 to mimic end user computers for testing purpose. Since R1 and R4 do not participate in EIGRP dynamic routing, we need to configure static routing on them.

   On R1, we configured a default route sending all outbound traffic to its directly connected neighbor's R2 (22.1.12.2). On R4, we configured a default route pointing to R3 (22.1.34.3).

```
R1(config)#ip route 0.0.0.0 0.0.0.0 22.1.12.2

R4(config)#ip route 0.0.0.0 0.0.0.0 22.1.34.3
```

5. **Finally make sure you have a fully working network, with no errors or warnings in "show logging". R1 can ping R4's Gig0/1 interface IP address, and so can R4 ping R1's Gig0/1 IP address.**

   Review the logs in "show logging" on all routers and make sure there is no error or warnings. On R1, ping R4 at 21.1.34.4.

```
R1#ping 22.1.34.4
Type escape sequence to abort.
Sending 5, 100-byte ICMP Echos to 22.1.34.4, timeout is 2 seconds:
!!!!!
Success rate is 100 percent (5/5), round-trip min/avg/max = 5/6/7 ms
R1#
```

   On R4, ping R1 at 22.1.12.1.

```
R4#ping 22.1.12.1
Type escape sequence to abort.
Sending 5, 100-byte ICMP Echos to 22.1.12.1, timeout is 2 seconds:
!!!!!
Success rate is 100 percent (5/5), round-trip min/avg/max = 3/4/6 ms
R4#
```

You just configured a fully converged network using EIGRP protocol.

6. Configure EIGRP for IPv6. Accomplish the same requirements as IPv4 outlined above.

Enable IPv6 unicast-routing and cef on all routers. Assign IPv6 addresses on all relevant interfaces. On R2 and R3, enable IPv6 EIGRP routing on participating interfaces.

On R2:

```
R2(config)#ipv6 unicast-routing
R2(config)#ipv6 cef
R2(config)#ipv6 router eigrp 100

R2(config)#interface Loopback0
R2(config-if)# ipv6 address 2001:2:2:2::2/128
R2(config-if)# ipv6 enable
R2(config-if)# ipv6 eigrp 100

R2(config-if)#interface GigabitEthernet0/1
R2(config-if)# ipv6 address 2001:22:1:12::2/64
R2(config-if)# ipv6 enable
R2(config-if)# ipv6 eigrp 100
R2#

R2(config-if)#interface GigabitEthernet0/2
R2(config-if)# ipv6 address 2001:22:1:23::2/64
R2(config-if)# ipv6 enable
R2(config-if)# ipv6 eigrp 100
R2#
```

On R3:

```
R3(config)#ipv6 unicast-routing
R3(config)#ipv6 cef
R3(config)#ipv6 router eigrp 100

R3(config)#interface Loopback0
R3(config-if)# ipv6 address 2001:3:3:3::3/128
```

```
R3(config-if)# ipv6 enable
R3(config-if)# ipv6 eigrp 100

R3(config-if)#interface GigabitEthernet0/1
R3(config-if)# ipv6 address 2001:22:1:23::3/64
R3(config-if)# ipv6 enable
R3(config-if)# ipv6 eigrp 100
R3#

R3(config-if)#interface GigabitEthernet0/2
R3(config-if)# ipv6 address 2001:22:1:34::3/64
R3(config-if)# ipv6 enable
R3(config-if)# ipv6 eigrp 100
R3#
```

R1 and R4 do not participate in IPv6 EIGRP routing but we still need to configure IPv6 static routing.

R1:

```
R1(config)#ipv6 unicast-routing
R1(config)#ipv6 cef

R1(config)#interface Loopback0
R1(config-if)# ipv6 address 2001:1:1:1::1/128
R1(config-if)# ipv6 enable

R1(config-if)#interface GigabitEthernet0/1
R1(config-if)# ipv6 address 2001:22:1:12::1/64
R1(config-if)# ipv6 enable

R1(config)# ipv6 route 2001::/16 2001:22:1:12::2
```

R4:

```
R4(config)#ipv6 unicast-routing
R4(config)#ipv6 cef

R4(config)#interface Loopback0
R4(config-if)# ipv6 address 2001:4:4:4::4/128
R4(config-if)# ipv6 enable

R4(config-if)#interface GigabitEthernet0/1
R4(config-if)# ipv6 address 2001:22:1:34::4/64
R4(config-if)# ipv6 enable
```

```
R4(config)# ipv6 route 2001::/16 2001:22:1:34::3
```

That's all the configurations needed. Next, we verify all the routing un IPv6 is working.

Confirm R2 and R3 have built IPv6 EIGRP neighbor relationship. Check IPv6 EIGRP routing table.

```
R2#show ipv6 eigrp neighbors
EIGRP-IPv6 Neighbors for AS(100)
H   Address                  Interface       Hold Uptime   SRTT   RTO  Q   Seq
                                             (sec)         (ms)        Cnt Num
0   Link-local address:      Gi0/2            12 00:07:03   11    100  0   3
    FE80::F816:3EFF:FE07:73F8
R2#
```

```
R2#sho ipv6 route eigrp
IPv6 Routing Table - default - 7 entries
Codes: C - Connected, L - Local, S - Static, U - Per-user Static route
       B - BGP, HA - Home Agent, MR - Mobile Router, R - RIP
       H - NHRP, I1 - ISIS L1, I2 - ISIS L2, IA - ISIS interarea
       IS - ISIS summary, D - EIGRP, EX - EIGRP external, NM - NEMO
       ND - ND Default, NDp - ND Prefix, DCE - Destination, NDr - Redirect
       RL - RPL, O - OSPF Intra, OI - OSPF Inter, OE1 - OSPF ext 1
       OE2 - OSPF ext 2, ON1 - OSPF NSSA ext 1, ON2 - OSPF NSSA ext 2
       la - LISP alt, lr - LISP site-registrations, ld - LISP dyn-eid
       lA - LISP away, a - Application
D   2001:3:3:3::3/128 [90/130816]
     via FE80::F816:3EFF:FE07:73F8, GigabitEthernet0/2
D   2001:22:1:34::/64 [90/3072]
     via FE80::F816:3EFF:FE07:73F8, GigabitEthernet0/2
R2#
```

Display IPv6 addresses on R1, R2, R3 and R4.

```
R1#show ipv6 int brief
GigabitEthernet0/0        [up/up]
    unassigned
GigabitEthernet0/1        [up/up]
    FE80::F816:3EFF:FE16:B838
    2001:22:1:12::1
Loopback0                 [up/up]
    FE80::5C00:FF:FE00:0
    2001:1:1:1::1
R1#
```

```
R2#show ipv6 interface brief
GigabitEthernet0/0        [up/up]
    unassigned
GigabitEthernet0/1        [up/up]
    FE80::F816:3EFF:FE39:FA71
    2001:22:1:12::2
GigabitEthernet0/2        [up/up]
    FE80::F816:3EFF:FED0:A044
    2001:22:1:23::2
Loopback0                 [up/up]
    FE80::5C00:FF:FE01:0
    2001:2:2:2::2
```

```
R3#show ipv6 interface brief
GigabitEthernet0/0          [up/up]
    unassigned
GigabitEthernet0/1          [up/up]
    FE80::F816:3EFF:FE07:73F8
    2001:22:1:23::3
GigabitEthernet0/2          [up/up]
    FE80::F816:3EFF:FED9:FD55
    2001:22:1:34::3
Loopback0                   [up/up]
    FE80::5C00:FF:FE02:0
    2001:3:3:3::3
```

```
R4#
R4#sho ipv6 int brief
GigabitEthernet0/0          [up/up]
    unassigned
GigabitEthernet0/1          [up/up]
    FE80::F816:3EFF:FE73:F925
    2001:22:1:34::4
Loopback0                   [up/up]
    FE80::5C00:FF:FE03:0
    2001:4:4:4::4
R4#
```

Make sure R1 can ping its directly connected R2.

```
R1#ping 2001:22:1:12::2
Type escape sequence to abort.
Sending 5, 100-byte ICMP Echos to 2001:22:1:12::2, timeout is 2 seconds:
!!!!!
Success rate is 100 percent (5/5), round-trip min/avg/max = 2/4/14 ms
R1#
```

On R1, ping R4. IPv6 EIGRP must be working for this ping to work.

```
R1#ping 2001:22:1:34::4
Type escape sequence to abort.
Sending 5, 100-byte ICMP Echos to 2001:22:1:34::4, timeout is 2 seconds:
!!!!!
Success rate is 100 percent (5/5), round-trip min/avg/max = 3/7/18 ms
R1#
```

You have completed all tasks in this Topology.

Topology 3: Configuring OSPF IPv4 and IPv6

Overview

The OSPF protocol is a link-state routing protocol, which means that the routers exchange topology information with their nearest neighbors. The topology information is flooded throughout the AS, so that every router within the AS has a complete picture of the topology of the AS. This picture is then used to calculate end-to-end paths through the AS, normally using a variant of the Dijkstra algorithm. Therefore, in a link-state routing protocol, the next hop address to which data is forwarded is determined by choosing the best end-to-end path to the eventual destination.

OSPF version 2 (OSPFv2) is used with IPv4. OSPFv3 has been updated for compatibility with IPv6's 128-bit address space. OSPF is also an open standard protocol, it is supported on Cisco and non-Cisco routers.

Network Topology

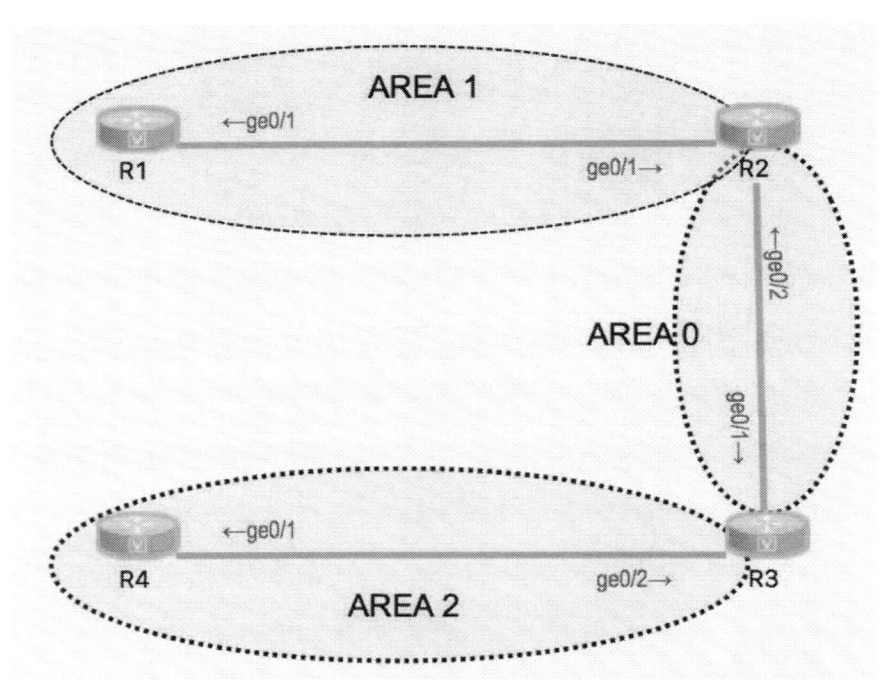

The network topology includes four routers. R2 and R3 represents the core network backbone in Area 0. R1 and R4 are remote and in Area 1 and Area 2 respectively.

What has been done in the initial configuration:

- Wiring among the switches and routers
- Host names
- OOB management IP addresses and loopback0 address
- Username / Password for switches and routers: cisco / cisco

Requirements

1. Configure OSPF on all routers with Area 0, 1 and 2 specified on the network diagram.

2. All routers shall advertise their directly connected interface subnets as well as their Loopback0 addresses to OSPF neighbors.

3. OSPF "router-id" shall be configured.

4. Finally make sure you have a fully converged network, with no errors or warnings in "show logging". All IPs shall be pingable by any router.

5. Configure OSPFv3 for IPv6. Accomplish the same requirements as IPv4 outlined above.

Solutions

1. Configure OSPF on all routers with Area 0, 1 and 2 specified on the network diagram.

Double click on the nodes to expand and show their physical layer connections. You can also use "show cdp neighbor" to view the neighbors directly connected to a particular router.

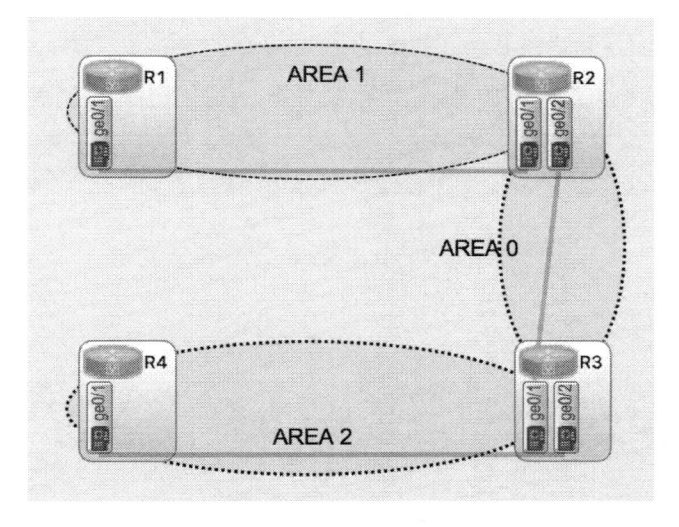

Configure R1 with OSPF routing. R1 is only participating in OSPF Area 1

```
R1(config)#router ospf 1
R1(config-router)# router-id 1.1.1.1
R1(config-router)# network 1.1.1.1 0.0.0.0 area 1
R1(config-router)# network 22.1.12.1 0.0.0.0 area 1
R1#
```

Configure R2 with OSPF routing. It is participating in Area 0 and Area 1.

```
R2(config)#router ospf 1
R2(config-router)# router-id 2.2.2.2
R2(config-router)# network 2.2.2.2 0.0.0.0 area 0
R2(config-router)# network 22.1.12.2 0.0.0.0 area 1
R2(config-router)# network 22.1.23.2 0.0.0.0 area 0
R2#
```

Configure R3 and R4 accordingly.

```
R3(config)#router ospf 1
R3(config-router)# router-id 3.3.3.3
R3(config-router)# network 3.3.3.3 0.0.0.0 area 0
R3(config-router)# network 22.1.23.3 0.0.0.0 area 0
R3(config-router)# network 22.1.34.3 0.0.0.0 area 2
R3#

R4(config)#router ospf 1
R4(config-router)# router-id 4.4.4.4
R4(config-router)# network 4.4.4.4 0.0.0.0 area 2
R4(config-router)# network 22.1.34.4 0.0.0.0 area 2
R4#
```

Logs show that OSPF adjacency is formed between routers.

```
R3#
*Jun  4 16:07:36.499: %SYS-5-CONFIG_I: Configured from console by console
*Jun  4 16:07:37.195: %OSPF-5-ADJCHG: Process 1, Nbr 2.2.2.2 on GigabitEthernet0/1 from LOADING to FULL, Loading Done
*Jun  4 16:08:31.456: %OSPF-5-ADJCHG: Process 1, Nbr 4.4.4.4 on GigabitEthernet0/2 from LOADING to FULL, Loading Done
R3#
```

Use "show ip ospf neighbor" command to display OSPF peers on all routers.

```
R1,R2,R3,R4#sho ip ospf neighbor
```

```
R2#sho ip ospf neighbor

Neighbor ID     Pri   State           Dead Time   Address         Interface
3.3.3.3           1   FULL/BDR        00:00:35    22.1.23.3       GigabitEthernet0/2
1.1.1.1           1   FULL/DR         00:00:39    22.1.12.1       GigabitEthernet0/1
R2#
```

```
R3#show ip ospf neighbor

Neighbor ID     Pri   State          Dead Time   Address      Interface
2.2.2.2           1   FULL/DR        00:00:38    22.1.23.2    GigabitEthernet0/1
4.4.4.4           1   FULL/BDR       00:00:33    22.1.34.4    GigabitEthernet0/2
R3#
```

2. All routers shall advertise their directly connected interface subnets as well as their Loopback0 addresses to OSPF neighbors.

   This configuration has been done in the previous step. For example, R1 has the following configuration.

```
router ospf 1
 network 1.1.1.1 0.0.0.0 area 1 !advertise loopback IP
 network 22.1.12.1 0.0.0.0 area 1 !advertise directly connected interface
```

3. OSPF "router-id" shall be configured.

   This configuration has been done in the previous step. For example, R1 has this configuration. Having "router-id" configured is a good idea when you are working on a large number of routers. When doing "show ip ospf neighbor", the "router-id" will be displayed. We can easily recognize that 1.1.1.1 is R1, 2.2.2.2 is R2 and so on.

```
router ospf 1
 router-id 1.1.1.1
```

4. Finally make sure you have a fully converged network, with no errors or warnings in "show logging". All IPs shall be pingable by any router.

   Review the routing tables on each router. Exam the OSPF routes that are in the routing table contains all the subnets advertised by other routers.

```
R1,R2,R3,R4#show ip route ospf
```

   Here is the OSPF routes on R1 should look like.

```
R1#show ip route ospf
Codes: L - local, C - connected, S - static, R - RIP, M - mobile, B - BGP
       D - EIGRP, EX - EIGRP external, O - OSPF, IA - OSPF inter area
       N1 - OSPF NSSA external type 1, N2 - OSPF NSSA external type 2
       E1 - OSPF external type 1, E2 - OSPF external type 2
       i - IS-IS, su - IS-IS summary, L1 - IS-IS level-1, L2 - IS-IS level-2
       ia - IS-IS inter area, * - candidate default, U - per-user static route
       o - ODR, P - periodic downloaded static route, H - NHRP, l - LISP
       a - application route
       + - replicated route, % - next hop override, p - overrides from PfR

Gateway of last resort is not set

      2.0.0.0/32 is subnetted, 1 subnets
O IA     2.2.2.2 [110/2] via 22.1.12.2, 00:27:57, GigabitEthernet0/1
      3.0.0.0/32 is subnetted, 1 subnets
O IA     3.3.3.3 [110/3] via 22.1.12.2, 00:26:32, GigabitEthernet0/1
      4.0.0.0/32 is subnetted, 1 subnets
O IA     4.4.4.4 [110/4] via 22.1.12.2, 00:25:38, GigabitEthernet0/1
      22.0.0.0/8 is variably subnetted, 4 subnets, 2 masks
O IA     22.1.23.0/24 [110/2] via 22.1.12.2, 00:27:57, GigabitEthernet0/1
O IA     22.1.34.0/24 [110/3] via 22.1.12.2, 00:26:32, GigabitEthernet0/1
R1#
```

Finally, now we have a fully converged network, meaning that anyone on the network should be able to reach to another peer. We want to ping all the IP addresses and make sure they are reachable.

Instead of pinging every IP address manually, we can use the TCL script to automate the ping to a list of IP addresses. The Cisco IOS Scripting with Tcl feature provides the ability to run Tool Command Language (Tcl) from the Cisco IOS command-line interface (CLI). Here is an example of the script. Fill in the IP addresses one per line and as many as you need. Copy & paste it into the router CLI and it'll be executed by pinging all the IPs listed.

(You can download workbook materials and scripts on www.speaknetworks.com)

```
tclsh
foreach ADDRESS {
1.1.1.1
2.2.2.2
3.3.3.3
4.4.4.4
22.1.12.1
22.1.12.2
22.1.23.2
22.1.23.3
22.1.34.3
22.1.34.4}
{ ping $ADDRESS }
```

```
R1#tclsh
R1(tcl)#foreach ADDRESS {
+>(tcl)#1.1.1.1
+>(tcl)#2.2.2.2
+>(tcl)#3.3.3.3
+>(tcl)#4.4.4.4
+>(tcl)#22.1.12.1
+>(tcl)#22.1.12.2
+>(tcl)#22.1.23.2
+>(tcl)#22.1.23.3
+>(tcl)#22.1.34.3
+>(tcl)#22.1.34.4
+>(tcl)#} { ping $ADDRESS }
Type escape sequence to abort.
Sending 5, 100-byte ICMP Echos to 1.1.1.1, timeout is 2 seconds:
!!!!!
Success rate is 100 percent (5/5), round-trip min/avg/max = 1/2/6 ms
Type escape sequence to abort.
Sending 5, 100-byte ICMP Echos to 2.2.2.2, timeout is 2 seconds:
!!!!!
Success rate is 100 percent (5/5), round-trip min/avg/max = 3/4/9 ms
Type escape sequence to abort.
Sending 5, 100-byte ICMP Echos to 3.3.3.3, timeout is 2 seconds:
!!!!!
Success rate is 100 percent (5/5), round-trip min/avg/max = 5/6/9 ms
Type escape sequence to abort.
Sending 5, 100-byte ICMP Echos to 4.4.4.4, timeout is 2 seconds:
!!!!!
Success rate is 100 percent (5/5), round-trip min/avg/max = 2/6/8 ms
```

Use this script on all the routers. Make sure the IP addresses are reachable.

> I found the Tcl script is extremely useful in CCIE labs when you have a large number of routers and IPs to verify reachability. Have it ready in a notepad and use it to confirm your network is working as expected before you are moving on to the next task is crucial to success.

5. Configure OSPFv3 for IPv6. Accomplish the same requirements as IPv4 outlined above.

Open Shortest Path First version 3 (OSPFv3) is an IPv4 and IPv6 link-state routing protocol that supports IPv6 and IPv4 unicast address families (AFs).

Comparison of OSPF V3 and OSPF V2 (reference Cisco.com)

- Much of OSPF version 3 is the same as in OSPF version 2. OSPFv3, which is described in RFC 5340, expands on OSPF version 2 to provide support for IPv6 routing prefixes and the larger size of IPv6 addresses.
- In OSPFv3, a routing process does not need to be explicitly created. Enabling OSPFv3 on an interface will cause a routing process, and its associated configuration, to be created.
- In OSPFv3, each interface must be enabled using commands in interface configuration mode. This feature is different from OSPF version 2, in which interfaces are indirectly enabled using the device configuration mode.

- When using a nonbroadcast multiaccess (NBMA) interface in OSPFv3, you must manually configure the device with the list of neighbors. Neighboring devices are identified by their device ID.
- In IPv6, you can configure many address prefixes on an interface. In OSPFv3, all address prefixes on an interface are included by default. You cannot select some address prefixes to be imported into OSPFv3; either all address prefixes on an interface are imported, or no address prefixes on an interface are imported.
- Unlike OSPF version 2, multiple instances of OSPFv3 can be run on a link.
- OSPF automatically prefers a loopback interface over any other kind, and it chooses the highest IP address among all loopback interfaces. If no loopback interfaces are present, the highest IP address in the device is chosen. You cannot tell OSPF to use any particular interface.

To configure OSPFv3 routing with IPv6, follow these 3 steps.

1. Enable IPv6 unicast routing on all routers
2. Enable IPv6 on the interfaces
3. Configure OSPFv3 under each participating interface

```
R1,R2,R3,R4(config)#ipv6 unicast-routing
R1,R2,R3,R4(config)#ipv6 cef
```

On R1:

```
R1(config)#ipv6 router ospf 1    !activate OSPFv3 process
R1(config-rtr)# router-id 1.1.1.1   !assign router-id

R1(config)#interface loopback0   !assign IPv6 address and enable OSPFv3 routing
R1(config-if)# ipv6 address 2001:1:1:1::1/128
R1(config-if)# ipv6 enable
R1(config-if)# ipv6 ospf 1 area 1

R1(config)#interface gig0/1
R1(config-if)# ipv6 address 2001:22:1:12::1/64
R1(config-if)# ipv6 enable
R1(config-if)# ipv6 ospf 1 area 1
R1#
```

On R2:

```
R2(config)#interface loopback0
R2(config-if)# ipv6 address 2001:2:2:2::2/128
```

```
R2(config-if)# ipv6 enable
R2(config-if)# ipv6 ospf 1 area 0

R2(config)#interface gig 0/1
R2(config-if)# ipv6 address 2001:22:1:12::2/64
R2(config-if)# ipv6 enable
R2(config-if)# ipv6 ospf 1 area 1

R2(config)#interface gig 0/2
R2(config-if)# ipv6 address 2001:22:1:23::2/64
R2(config-if)# ipv6 enable
R2(config-if)# ipv6 ospf 1 area 0

R2(config)#ipv6 router ospf 1
R2(config-rtr)# router-id 2.2.2.2
R2#
```

On R3:

```
R3(config)#interface loopback0
R3(config-if)# ipv6 address 2001:3:3:3::3/128
R3(config-if)# ipv6 enable
R3(config-if)# ipv6 ospf 1 area 0

R3(config-if)#interface gig 0/1
R3(config-if)# ipv6 address 2001:22:1:23::3/64
R3(config-if)# ipv6 enable
R3(config-if)# ipv6 ospf 1 area 0

R3(config-if)#interface gig 0/2
R3(config-if)# ipv6 address 2001:22:1:34::3/64
R3(config-if)# ipv6 enable
R3(config-if)# ipv6 ospf 1 area 2

R3(config)#ipv6 router ospf 1
R3(config-rtr)# router-id 3.3.3.3
R3#
```

On R4:

```
R4(config)#interface loopback0
R4(config-if)# ipv6 address 2001:4:4:4::4/128
R4(config-if)# ipv6 enable
R4(config-if)# ipv6 ospf 1 area 2

R4(config)#interface gig0/1
R4(config-if)# ipv6 address 2001:22:1:34::4/64
```

```
R4(config-if)# ipv6 enable
R4(config-if)# ipv6 ospf 1 area 2

R4(config)#ipv6 router ospf 1
R4(config-rtr)# router-id 4.4.4.4
R4#
```

Check OSPFv3 adjacencies on R2 and R3. Make sure use "ipv6" in the commands.

```
R2,R3#show ipv6 ospf neighbor
```

```
R2#show ipv6 ospf neighbor

            OSPFv3 Router with ID (2.2.2.2) (Process ID 1)

Neighbor ID     Pri   State          Dead Time   Interface ID    Interface
3.3.3.3           1   FULL/BDR       00:00:34    3               GigabitEthernet0/2
1.1.1.1           1   FULL/DR        00:00:34    3               GigabitEthernet0/1
R2#
```

```
R3#show ipv6 ospf neighbor

            OSPFv3 Router with ID (3.3.3.3) (Process ID 1)

Neighbor ID     Pri   State          Dead Time   Interface ID    Interface
2.2.2.2           1   FULL/DR        00:00:37    4               GigabitEthernet0/1
4.4.4.4           1   FULL/BDR       00:00:31    3               GigabitEthernet0/2
R3#
```

Verify IPv6 routing tables on each router and confirm all IPv6 subnets that are participating in OSPFv3 routing are present.

```
R1,R2,R3,R4#show ipv6 route ospf
```

Here is you should see on R1.

```
R1#show ipv6 route ospf
IPv6 Routing Table - default - 9 entries
Codes: C - Connected, L - Local, S - Static, U - Per-user Static route
       B - BGP, HA - Home Agent, MR - Mobile Router, R - RIP
       H - NHRP, I1 - ISIS L1, I2 - ISIS L2, IA - ISIS interarea
       IS - ISIS summary, D - EIGRP, EX - EIGRP external, NM - NEMO
       ND - ND Default, NDp - ND Prefix, DCE - Destination, NDr - Redirect
       RL - RPL, O - OSPF Intra, OI - OSPF Inter, OE1 - OSPF ext 1
       OE2 - OSPF ext 2, ON1 - OSPF NSSA ext 1, ON2 - OSPF NSSA ext 2
       la - LISP alt, lr - LISP site-registrations, ld - LISP dyn-eid
       lA - LISP away, a - Application
OI  2001:2:2:2::2/128 [110/1]
     via FE80::F816:3EFF:FE77:843, GigabitEthernet0/1
OI  2001:3:3:3::3/128 [110/2]
     via FE80::F816:3EFF:FE77:843, GigabitEthernet0/1
OI  2001:4:4:4::4/128 [110/3]
     via FE80::F816:3EFF:FE77:843, GigabitEthernet0/1
OI  2001:22:1:23::/64 [110/2]
     via FE80::F816:3EFF:FE77:843, GigabitEthernet0/1
OI  2001:22:1:34::/64 [110/3]
     via FE80::F816:3EFF:FE77:843, GigabitEthernet0/1
R1#
```

Lastly, let's do some IPv6 ping testing. (you can download workbook materials and scripts on www.speaknetworks.com)

```
tclsh
foreach ADDRESS {
2001:1:1:1::1
2001:2:2:2::2
2001:3:3:3::3
2001:4:4:4::4
2001:22:1:12::1
2001:22:1:12::2
2001:22:1:23::2
2001:22:1:23::3
2001:22:1:34::3
2001:22:1:34::4
} { ping $ADDRESS }
```

```
R1#tclsh
R1(tcl)#foreach ADDRESS {
+>(tcl)#2001:1:1:1::1
+>(tcl)#2001:2:2:2::2
+>(tcl)#2001:3:3:3::3
+>(tcl)#2001:4:4:4::4
+>(tcl)#2001:22:1:12::1
+>(tcl)#2001:22:1:12::2
+>(tcl)#2001:22:1:23::2
+>(tcl)#2001:22:1:23::3
+>(tcl)#2001:22:1:34::3
+>(tcl)#2001:22:1:34::4
+>(tcl)#} { ping $ADDRESS }
Type escape sequence to abort.
Sending 5, 100-byte ICMP Echos to 2001:1:1:1::1, timeout is 2 seconds:
!!!!!
Success rate is 100 percent (5/5), round-trip min/avg/max = 1/1/4 ms
Type escape sequence to abort.
Sending 5, 100-byte ICMP Echos to 2001:2:2:2::2, timeout is 2 seconds:
!!!!!
Success rate is 100 percent (5/5), round-trip min/avg/max = 2/3/6 ms
Type escape sequence to abort.
Sending 5, 100-byte ICMP Echos to 2001:3:3:3::3, timeout is 2 seconds:
!!!!!
Success rate is 100 percent (5/5), round-trip min/avg/max = 2/4/10 ms
Type escape sequence to abort.
Sending 5, 100-byte ICMP Echos to 2001:4:4:4::4, timeout is 2 seconds:
!!!!!
```

Congratulations, you have completed all tasks in this Topology.

Topology 4: Configuring IOS NAT/PAT

Overview

Network Address Translation (NAT) is designed for IP address conservation. It enables private IP networks that use unregistered IP addresses to connect to the Internet. NAT operates on a router, usually connecting two networks together, and translates the private (not globally unique) addresses in the internal network into legal addresses, before packets are forwarded to another network.

As part of this capability, NAT can be configured to advertise only one address for the entire network to the outside world. This provides additional security by effectively hiding the entire internal network behind that address. NAT offers the dual functions of security and address conservation and is typically implemented in remote-access environments.

In this lab, we'll setup a simple network consisting of a router (R1), bridging between private corporate network (192.168.1.0/24) and the public Internet (200.1.1.0/24). For simplicity, only two subnets and one router are involved.

You will also learn how to setup a non-networking device such as a Linux server in VIRL.

Network Topology

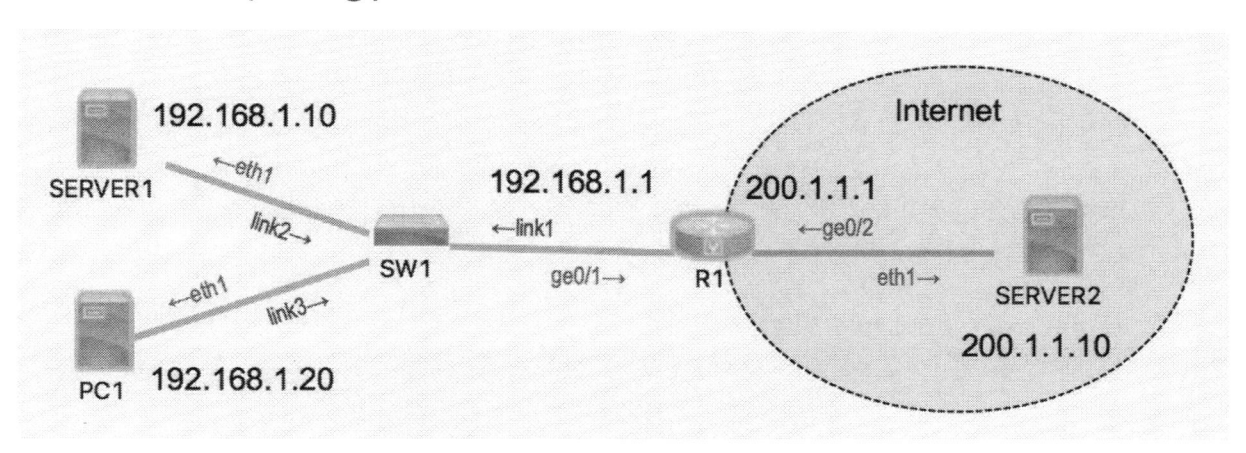

The network topology includes a router, a layer 2 switch and three Linux servers.

What has been done in the initial configuration:

- Wiring among the switches and routers
- Host names
- Basic configuration of R1 and Server IP addresses
- OOB management IP addresses
- Username / Password for switches and routers and servers: cisco / cisco

Requirements

1. Configure basic static routing on R1 so that its default gateway pointing to SERVER2.

2. Configure NAT Overload on R1 so that internal hosts (SERVER1 and PC1) use R1's Internet facing IP to reach SERVER2.

3. Configure NAT on R1 so that SERVER2 on the Internet may reach the internal SERVER1 using Public IP 200.1.1.2 on TCP 80 and 443.

4. Finally make sure you have a fully working network, with no errors or warnings in "show logging".

5. As results, PC1 and SERVER1 can ping SERVER2. And SERVER2 may reach SERVER1 over port 80 and 443.

Solutions

0. How Linux servers are configured

> The topology files (initial.virl and final.virl) come with the workbook already have Linux servers preconfigured. This section is for your information. You may skip to the first requirement.

VIRL supports not only Cisco devices, it also supports 3rd party virtual machines. For example, Linux (Ubuntu) server. AutoNetkit is used to generate the initial configuration for all nodes. This is especially important if you are running any "server" subtype nodes. AutoNetkit generates the initial booting configuration for the Linux servers. You won't be able to login to a Linux server without going through the AutoNetkit auto-config.

Configure Server IPs and Routing

If you have any "server" in your topology, you may configure the server's IP address and routing table before launching. Here is an example. We are setting up Server 1 with one network interface "eth1". IP address 192.168.1.10 /24 is assigned to its NIC. We have also configured a default gateway on the server that is pointing to R1 (192.168.1.1) directly connected. See below configuration snippets for Server 1, PC1 and Server 2. It is part of the ".virl" topology file. As you have found, they are basic Linux commands assigning IP address to interface and adding static routes to the routing table.

Server 1:

```
content: |-
   #!/bin/sh
   ifconfig eth1 up 192.168.1.10 netmask 255.255.255.0
   route add -net 0.0.0.0 netmask 0.0.0.0 gw 192.168.1.1 dev eth1
exit 0
```

PC1:

```
content: |-
   ifconfig eth1 up 192.168.1.20 netmask 255.255.255.0
   route add -net 0.0.0.0 netmask 0.0.0.0 gw 192.168.1.1 dev eth1
exit 0
```

Server 2:

```
content: |-
   ifconfig eth1 up 200.1.1.10 netmask 255.255.255.0
   route add -net 0.0.0.0 netmask 0.0.0.0 gw 200.1.1.1 dev eth1
exit 0
```

Here is how the ".virl" topology file looks like.

```
      <node name="SERVER1" type="SIMPLE" subtype="server" location="82,115">
         <extensions>
            <entry key="config" type="String">#cloud-config
bootcmd:
- ln -s -t /etc/rc.d /etc/rc.local
hostname: SERVER1
manage_etc_hosts: true
runcmd:
- start ttyS0
- systemctl start getty@ttyS0.service
- systemctl start rc-local
- sed -i '/^\s*PasswordAuthentication\s\+no/d' /etc/ssh/sshd_config
- echo "UseDNS no" &gt;&gt; /etc/ssh/sshd_config
- service ssh restart
- service sshd restart
users:
- default
- gecos: User configured by VIRL Configuration Engine 0.23.7
  lock-passwd: false
  name: cisco
  plain-text-passwd: cisco
  shell: /bin/bash
  ssh-authorized-keys:
  - VIRL-USER-SSH-PUBLIC-KEY
  sudo: ALL=(ALL) ALL
write_files:
- path: /etc/init/ttyS0.conf
  owner: root:root
  content: |
```

```
      - path: /etc/systemd/system/dhclient@.service
        content: |
          [Unit]
          Description=Run dhclient on %i interface
          After=network.target
          [Service]
          Type=oneshot
          ExecStart=/sbin/dhclient %i -pf /var/run/dhclient.%i.pid -lf
          /var/lib/dhclient/dhclient.%i.lease
          RemainAfterExit=yes
        owner: root:root
        permissions: '0644'
      - path: /etc/rc.local
        owner: root:root
        permissions: '0755'
        content: |-
          #!/bin/sh
          ifconfig eth1 up 192.168.1.10 netmask 255.255.255.0
          route add -net 0.0.0.0 netmask 0.0.0.0 gw 192.168.1.1 dev eth1
          exit 0
</entry>
```

If you downloaded the workbook topology files, the server configuration has been done for you. Launch the topology without changing anything. Let's validate the servers.

On SERVER 1, verify its IP address and routing table. Confirm it can ping R1 at 192.168.1.1.

```
cisco@SERVER1:~$ ifconfig eth1
cisco@SERVER1:~$ netstat -rn
```

```
cisco@SERVER1:~$ ifconfig eth1
eth1      Link encap:Ethernet  HWaddr fa:16:3e:06:1f:09
          inet addr:192.168.1.10  Bcast:192.168.1.255  Mask:255.255.255.0
          inet6 addr: fe80::f816:3eff:fe06:1f09/64 Scope:Link
          UP BROADCAST RUNNING MULTICAST  MTU:1500  Metric:1
          RX packets:89 errors:0 dropped:72 overruns:0 frame:0
          TX packets:10 errors:0 dropped:0 overruns:0 carrier:0
          collisions:0 txqueuelen:1000
          RX bytes:27351 (27.3 KB)  TX bytes:788 (788.0 B)

cisco@SERVER1:~$ netstat -rn
Kernel IP routing table
Destination     Gateway         Genmask         Flags   MSS Window  irtt Iface
0.0.0.0         192.168.1.1     0.0.0.0         UG        0 0          0 eth1
0.0.0.0         172.16.1.254    0.0.0.0         UG        0 0          0 eth0
172.16.1.0      0.0.0.0         255.255.255.0   U         0 0          0 eth0
192.168.1.0     0.0.0.0         255.255.255.0   U         0 0          0 eth1
cisco@SERVER1:~$
```

```
cisco@SERVER1:~$ ping 192.168.1.1
PING 192.168.1.1 (192.168.1.1) 56(84) bytes of data.
64 bytes from 192.168.1.1: icmp_seq=1 ttl=255 time=2.69 ms
64 bytes from 192.168.1.1: icmp_seq=2 ttl=255 time=2.39 ms
64 bytes from 192.168.1.1: icmp_seq=3 ttl=255 time=2.52 ms
^C
--- 192.168.1.1 ping statistics ---
3 packets transmitted, 3 received, 0% packet loss, time 2003ms
rtt min/avg/max/mdev = 2.396/2.536/2.690/0.127 ms
cisco@SERVER1:~$
```

Validate the same on SERVER 2.

```
cisco@SERVER2:~$ netstat -rn
Kernel IP routing table
Destination     Gateway         Genmask         Flags   MSS Window  irtt Iface
0.0.0.0         200.1.1.1       0.0.0.0         UG        0 0          0 eth1
0.0.0.0         172.16.1.254    0.0.0.0         UG        0 0          0 eth0
172.16.1.0      0.0.0.0         255.255.255.0   U         0 0          0 eth0
200.1.1.0       0.0.0.0         255.255.255.0   U         0 0          0 eth1
cisco@SERVER2:~$
cisco@SERVER2:~$ ping 200.1.1.1
PING 200.1.1.1 (200.1.1.1) 56(84) bytes of data.
64 bytes from 200.1.1.1: icmp_seq=1 ttl=255 time=3.53 ms
64 bytes from 200.1.1.1: icmp_seq=2 ttl=255 time=3.01 ms
64 bytes from 200.1.1.1: icmp_seq=3 ttl=255 time=2.85 ms
^C
--- 200.1.1.1 ping statistics ---
3 packets transmitted, 3 received, 0% packet loss, time 2003ms
rtt min/avg/max/mdev = 2.851/3.134/3.537/0.296 ms
cisco@SERVER2:~$ ifconfig eth1
eth1      Link encap:Ethernet  HWaddr fa:16:3e:3a:65:1e
          inet addr:200.1.1.10  Bcast:200.1.1.255  Mask:255.255.255.0
          inet6 addr: fe80::f816:3eff:fe3a:651e/64 Scope:Link
          UP BROADCAST RUNNING MULTICAST  MTU:1500  Metric:1
          RX packets:92 errors:0 dropped:77 overruns:0 frame:0
          TX packets:13 errors:0 dropped:0 overruns:0 carrier:0
          collisions:0 txqueuelen:1000
          RX bytes:29234 (29.2 KB)  TX bytes:1082 (1.0 KB)

cisco@SERVER2:~$
```

You are ready to move on to the first requirement.

1. Configure basic static routing on R1 so that its default gateway pointing to SERVER2.

Use "ip route" command to configure a static route on R1. Ensure it can ping SERVER 2.

```
ip route 0.0.0.0 0.0.0.0 200.1.1.10
```

```
R1#sho ip route static
Codes: L - local, C - connected, S - static, R - RIP, M - mobile, B - BGP
       D - EIGRP, EX - EIGRP external, O - OSPF, IA - OSPF inter area
       N1 - OSPF NSSA external type 1, N2 - OSPF NSSA external type 2
       E1 - OSPF external type 1, E2 - OSPF external type 2
       i - IS-IS, su - IS-IS summary, L1 - IS-IS level-1, L2 - IS-IS level-2
       ia - IS-IS inter area, * - candidate default, U - per-user static route
       o - ODR, P - periodic downloaded static route, H - NHRP, l - LISP
       a - application route
       + - replicated route, % - next hop override, p - overrides from PfR

Gateway of last resort is 200.1.1.10 to network 0.0.0.0

S*    0.0.0.0/0 [1/0] via 200.1.1.10
R1#
R1#
R1#
R1#ping 200.1.1.10
Type escape sequence to abort.
Sending 5, 100-byte ICMP Echos to 200.1.1.10, timeout is 2 seconds:
!!!!!
Success rate is 100 percent (5/5), round-trip min/avg/max = 3/4/8 ms
R1#
```

2. Configure NAT Overload on R1 so that internal hosts (SERVER1 and PC1) use R1's Internet facing IP to reach SERVER2

First, define NAT inside and outside interfaces. On R1, Gig0/1 is the inside facing interface. We make it NAT "inside". On the other hand, the Gig 0/2 is Internet facing interface. We make it NAT "outside". It doesn't really matter which side you make it inside or outside; the NAT configuration can be reversed. Naturally, we define the private internal network as "inside".

```
interface GigabitEthernet0/1
 description to SW1
 ip address 192.168.1.1 255.255.255.0
 ip nat inside
 duplex full
 speed auto
!
interface GigabitEthernet0/2
 description to SERVER2
 ip address 200.1.1.1 255.255.255.0
 ip nat outside
 duplex full
 speed auto
```

Second, configure an ACL (Access Control List) to classify what inside subnets will be translated using the NAT.

```
access-list 100 permit ip 192.168.1.0 0.0.0.255 any
```

Access-list 100 states, any traffic sourced from 192.168.1.0/24 destined to anywhere (Internet), qualifies this access-list. Furthermore, IP address translation will be applied by the NAT commands.

```
ip nat inside source list 100 interface GigabitEthernet0/2 overload
```

The "interface" argument lets the NAT use Gig 0/2's IP address to translate the 192.168.1.0/24 addresses when outbound to the Internet.

The "overload" argument allows multiple users/IPs to be mapped to the same public IP, in this case, it is the Gig 0/2 interface IP.

What this requirement has accomplished is that, it configured a NAT rule which enables internal hosts on the LAN 192.168.1.0/24 to access the Internet subnet 200.1.1.0/24 by converting their non-Internet routable IPs (192.168.1.x) to Internet routable IP (200.1.1.1).

3. Configure NAT on R1 so that SERVER2 on the Internet may reach the internal SERVER1 using Public IP 200.1.1.2 on TCP 80 and 443

This requirement is to mimic the environment where you have a Webserver (SERVER 1) on your internal network. You need to allow inbound access from the Internet to it on TCP HTTP (80) and HTTPS (443). You'll provide the public IP 200.1.1.2 to the Internet users to access the Webserver.

```
ip nat inside source static tcp 192.168.1.10 80 200.1.1.2 80 extendable
ip nat inside source static tcp 192.168.1.10 443 200.1.1.2 443 extendable
```

The NAT configuration states, traffic coming from the Internet destined to 200.1.1.2 over port 80 and 443, translate the destination IP to 192.168.1.10 and forward on based on the router's routing table.

R1 already has Gig 0/1 connected to the 192.168.1.0/24 network. It wouldn't be hard for it to find SERVER 1 on 192.168.1.10.

Return traffic will be "translated back" based on the same NAT statements in reverse order.

Note that a router is not a firewall. This lab setup is to simplify the environment so that we can focus on Cisco IOS router's functionalities. In real-world production environment, an Internet boundary Firewall such as Cisco ASA is deployed. The Webserver shall be setup in a DMZ security zone of the Firewall, which provides additional protection to internal resources in case the Webserver is compromised.

4. Finally make sure you have a fully working network, with no errors or warnings in "show logging"

Use "show logging" on R1 to verify that there is no error in the logs.

```
R1#show logging
```

5. As results, PC1 and SERVER1 can ping SERVER2. And SERVER2 may reach SERVER1 over port 80 and 443.

To validate the result for requirement #2, login PC1 and initiate a continuous ping towards the Internet host SERVER 2 (200.1.1.2).

```
cisco@PC1:~$ ping 200.1.1.2
PING 200.1.1.2 (200.1.1.2) 56(84) bytes of data.
64 bytes from 200.1.1.2: icmp_seq=1 ttl=255 time=3.99 ms
64 bytes from 200.1.1.2: icmp_seq=2 ttl=255 time=2.39 ms
64 bytes from 200.1.1.2: icmp_seq=3 ttl=255 time=2.44 ms
64 bytes from 200.1.1.2: icmp_seq=4 ttl=255 time=2.33 ms
64 bytes from 200.1.1.2: icmp_seq=5 ttl=255 time=2.95 ms
64 bytes from 200.1.1.2: icmp_seq=6 ttl=255 time=3.02 ms
64 bytes from 200.1.1.2: icmp_seq=7 ttl=255 time=2.47 ms
```

It proves the routing and NAT are working. Let's see what R1 is doing.

```
R1#show ip nat translations
```

```
R1#show ip nat translations
Pro Inside global      Inside local        Outside local      Outside global
tcp 200.1.1.2:80       192.168.1.10:80     ---                ---
tcp 200.1.1.2:443      192.168.1.10:443    ---                ---
icmp 200.1.1.1:1494    192.168.1.20:1494   200.1.1.2:1494     200.1.1.2:1494
```

As you can see the bottom line of the output, R1 translated PC1's IP 192.168.1.20 to its own Gig 0/1 200.1.1.1 and used it to talk to SERVER 2 at 200.1.1.2. The protocol is "icmp" which is used by ping.

The first two lines represent static NAT configuration over port 80 and 443. Note that with access-list-based NAT, the process creates one "parent" IP-to-IP address translation entry, which is used to multiplex all sessions for this particular inside host. Those IP-to-IP entries are called non-extendable because they only have inside local and inside global IP address information. The one-to-one entries also permit outside hosts to connect to the inside using the temporary mapped IP address. Additionally, with non-extendable entries, an inside local address may have only one inside global translation. This effectively prevents multi-homed NAT when using access-lists only for NAT configuration.

Lastly, we need to test requirement #3 and make sure Internet users can reach the Webserver over port 80 and 443. To simulate user traffic, we can login SERVER 2 and try Telnet 200.1.1.2 over port 80 and 443. Let's ping it first.

```
cisco@SERVER2:~$ ping 200.1.1.2
```

```
cisco@SERVER2:~$
cisco@SERVER2:~$ ping 200.1.1.2
PING 200.1.1.2 (200.1.1.2) 56(84) bytes of data.
64 bytes from 200.1.1.2: icmp_seq=1 ttl=255 time=5.43 ms
64 bytes from 200.1.1.2: icmp_seq=2 ttl=255 time=2.87 ms
^C
--- 200.1.1.2 ping statistics ---
2 packets transmitted, 2 received, 0% packet loss, time 1001ms
rtt min/avg/max/mdev = 2.873/4.154/5.436/1.283 ms
cisco@SERVER2:~$
```

```
cisco@SERVER2:~$ telnet 200.1.1.2 80
cisco@SERVER2:~$ telnet 200.1.1.2 443
```

```
cisco@SERVER2:~$ telnet 200.1.1.2 80
Trying 200.1.1.2...
telnet: Unable to connect to remote host: Connection refused
cisco@SERVER2:~$ telnet 200.1.1.2 443
Trying 200.1.1.2...
telnet: Unable to connect to remote host: Connection refused
cisco@SERVER2:~$
```

It shows connection refused because SERVER 1 does not have web services setup. If we were to configure and run web services on SERVER 1, Telnet will connect.

Log in R1 and review NAT transactions. Now two new entries have shown up in result of the Telnet attempts.

```
R1#show ip nat translations
Pro Inside global      Inside local        Outside local       Outside global
tcp 200.1.1.2:80       192.168.1.10:80     200.1.1.10:45936    200.1.1.10:45936
tcp 200.1.1.2:80       192.168.1.10:80     ---                 ---
tcp 200.1.1.2:443      192.168.1.10:443    200.1.1.10:59550    200.1.1.10:59550
tcp 200.1.1.2:443      192.168.1.10:443    ---                 ---
icmp 200.1.1.1:1494    192.168.1.20:1494   200.1.1.2:1494      200.1.1.2:1494
R1#
```

At this point we have a fully working network. Congratulations, you have completed this topology.

Topology 5: Configuring ASA with Multiple DMZ Networks (Security)

Overview

Do you have any public facing web servers on your network? Do you have guest Wi-Fi enabled but you do not want visitors to access your internal resource? In this lab we'll learn about security segmentations by creating multiple security levels on a Cisco ASA firewall. The network diagram below illustrates common network requirements in a corporate environment.

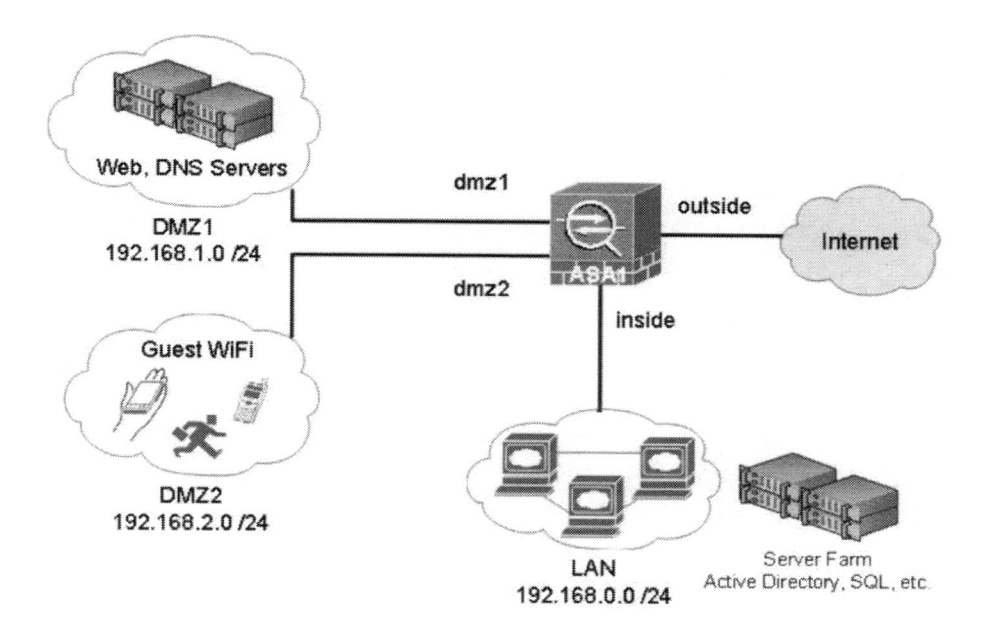

A Cisco ASA is deployed as an Internet gateway, providing outbound Internet access to all internal hosts. There are four security levels configured on the ASA, LAN, DMZ1, DMZ2 and outside. Their security level from high to low is as following: LAN > DMZ1 > DMZ2 > outside.

- LAN is considered the most secured network. It not only hosts internal user workstations as well as mission critical production servers. LAN users can reach other networks. However, no inbound access is allowed from any other networks unless explicitly allowed.
- DMZ1 hosts public facing web servers. Any one on the Internet can reach the servers on TCP port 80. DMZ1 also hosts DNS servers for guest Wi-Fi in DMZ2.

- DMZ2 is designed as untrusted guest network. Its sole purpose is providing Internet access for visitors. For Internet content filtering, they are required to use the in-house DNS servers in DMZ1.

The design idea here is that we don't allow any possibilities of compromising the LAN. All "inbound" access to the LAN is denied unless the connection is initiated from the inside hosts. Servers in DMZ1 have two purposes, serving Internet web traffic and DNS resolution queries from DMZ2, the guest Wi-Fi network. We do have DNS servers on the LAN for internal users and servers. But we do not want to open any firewall holes to our most secured network. The worst-case assumption is that, in case DMZ2 is compromised since it is the least controlled network, it can potentially impact DMZ1 because we do have a firewall rules open for DNS access from DMZ2 to DMZ1. Suppose both DMZ1 and DMZ2 are compromised, and the hacker has no way making his way into the LAN subnet because no firewall rules allow any access into the LAN whatsoever.

Security levels on Cisco ASA Firewall

By default, traffic passing from a lower to higher security level is denied. This can be overridden by an ACL applied to that lower security interface. Also the ASA, by default, will allow traffic from higher to lower security interfaces. This behavior can also be overridden with an ACL. The security levels are defined by numeric numbers between 0 and 100. 0 is often placed on the untrusted network such as Internet. And 100 is the most secured network. In our configuration we assign security levels as following: LAN = 100, DMZ1 = 50, DMZ2 = 20 and outside = 0.

The information in this lab applies to the latest ASA-5500-X series with FirePower Services running ASA code (not FTD), and legacy Cisco ASA 5500 series running code 8.3 and later.

Network Topology

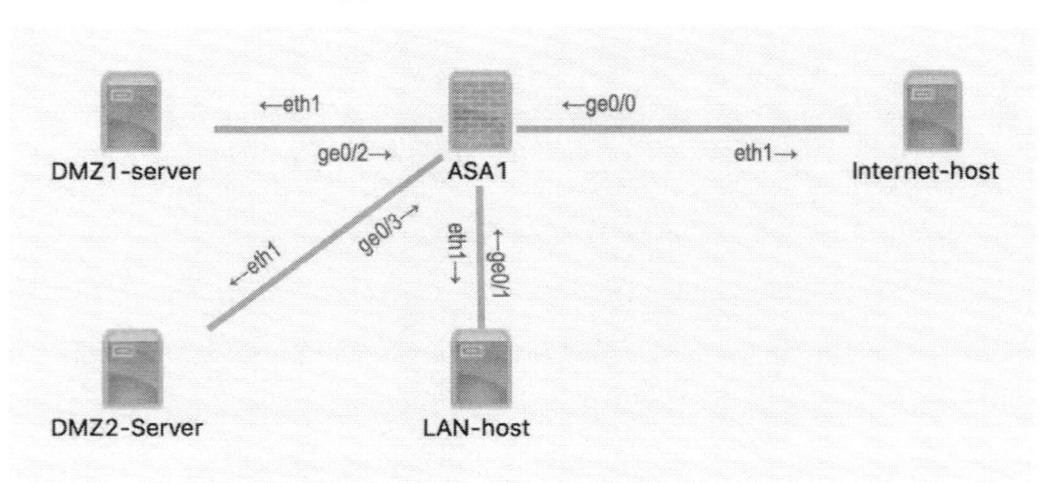

The network topology includes four Linux servers and one Cisco ASA. The Linux servers are there to mimic real-world user computers and servers. They can be used to perform Ping and Traceroute testing.

What has been done in the initial configuration:

- Wiring among the switches and routers
- Host names, static IP addresses and default gateways pointing to the ASA.
- OOB management IP addresses
- Username / Password for servers and ASA: cisco / cisco

Requirements

1. Set up four security levels on the ASA: LAN, DMZ1, DMZ2 and outside. Security levels from high to low: LAN > DMZ1 > DMZ2 > outside.

2. A Cisco ASA is deployed as an Internet gateway, providing outbound Internet access to all internal hosts.

3. Configure static NAT to the web server, grant Internet inbound access to web server.

4. Enforce Inter-security segment access control.

   o DMZ1 hosts public facing web servers. Any one on the Internet can reach the servers on TCP port 80. DMZ1 also hosts DNS servers for guest Wi-Fi in DMZ2.

   o DMZ2 is designed as an untrusted guest network. Its sole purpose is providing Internet access for visitors. For Internet content filtering, they are required to use the in-house DNS servers in DMZ1.

5. Finally make sure you have a fully working network, with no errors or warnings in "show logging" on the ASA.

Solutions

1. Validate initial configuration.

Before we configure the ASA, let's first validate all the Linux servers have come up with their IPs assigned and they can ping the ASA as a gateway.

Below is the configuration of "LAN-host". We assigned an IP 192.168.0.200/24 on its ETH1 interface. Two static routes were added to the server's routing table to help reaching the hosts in other security zones.

```
#!/bin/sh
    ifconfig eth1 up 192.168.0.200 netmask 255.255.255.0
    route add -net 10.1.1.0 netmask 255.255.255.0 gw 192.168.0.1 dev eth1
    route add -net 192.168.0.0 netmask 255.255.0.0 gw 192.168.0.1 dev eth1
exit 0
```

Here are the commands you can use to validate network connectivity and the expected results.

```
cisco@LAN-host:~$ ifconfig eth1
cisco@LAN-host:~$ netstat -rn
cisco@LAN-host:~$ ping 192.168.0.1
```

```
cisco@LAN-host:~$ ifconfig eth1
eth1      Link encap:Ethernet  HWaddr fa:16:3e:d1:e0:a0
          inet addr:192.168.0.200  Bcast:192.168.0.255  Mask:255.255.255.0
          inet6 addr: fe80::f816:3eff:fed1:e0a0/64 Scope:Link
          UP BROADCAST RUNNING MULTICAST  MTU:1500  Metric:1
          RX packets:3 errors:0 dropped:0 overruns:0 frame:0
          TX packets:10 errors:0 dropped:0 overruns:0 carrier:0
          collisions:0 txqueuelen:1000
          RX bytes:256 (256.0 B)  TX bytes:788 (788.0 B)

cisco@LAN-host:~$ netstat -rn
Kernel IP routing table
Destination     Gateway         Genmask         Flags   MSS Window  irtt Iface
0.0.0.0         10.255.0.1      0.0.0.0         UG       0 0          0 eth0
10.1.1.0        192.168.0.1     255.255.255.0   UG       0 0          0 eth1
10.255.0.0      0.0.0.0         255.255.0.0     U        0 0          0 eth0
169.254.169.254 10.255.0.1      255.255.255.255 UGH      0 0          0 eth0
192.168.0.0     0.0.0.0         255.255.255.0   U        0 0          0 eth1
192.168.0.0     192.168.0.1     255.255.0.0     UG       0 0          0 eth1
cisco@LAN-host:~$ ping 192.168.0.1
PING 192.168.0.1 (192.168.0.1) 56(84) bytes of data.
64 bytes from 192.168.0.1: icmp_seq=1 ttl=255 time=1.81 ms
64 bytes from 192.168.0.1: icmp_seq=2 ttl=255 time=1.42 ms
64 bytes from 192.168.0.1: icmp_seq=3 ttl=255 time=1.73 ms
^C
--- 192.168.0.1 ping statistics ---
3 packets transmitted, 3 received, 0% packet loss, time 2003ms
rtt min/avg/max/mdev = 1.423/1.657/1.816/0.175 ms
cisco@LAN-host:~$
```

"Lan-host" has stood up with the correct IP address and it can ping the ASA192.168.0.1. Review every server and make sure they have booted up with fully network connectivity. On ASA1, display all the interface IP addresses.

```
ASA1# show ip
```

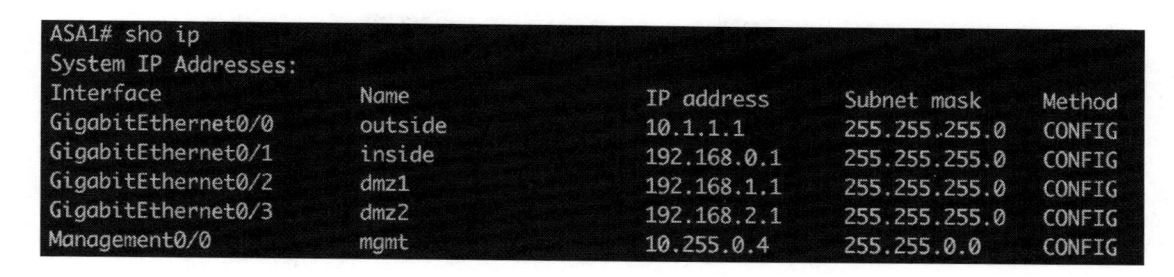

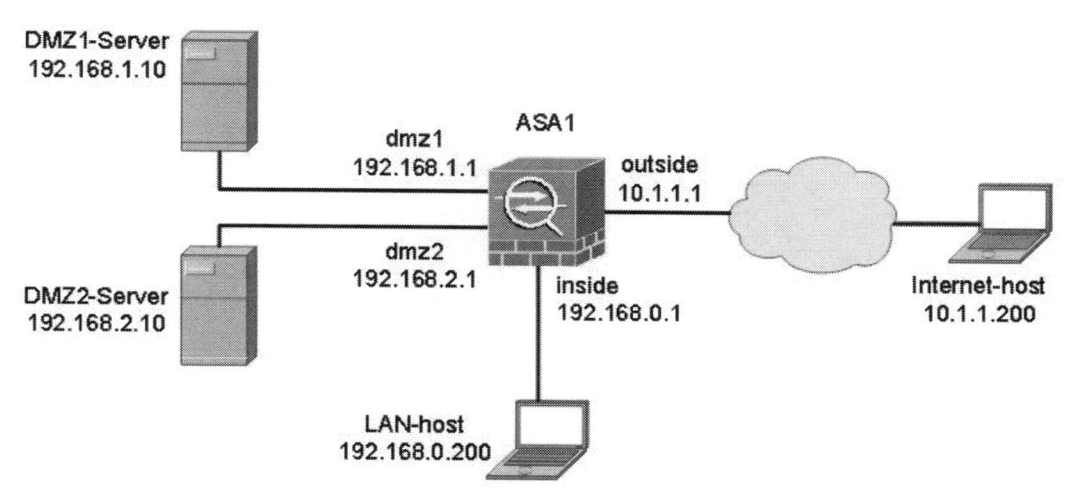

```
ASA1# sho ip
System IP Addresses:
Interface                Name          IP address        Subnet mask        Method
GigabitEthernet0/0       outside       10.1.1.1          255.255.255.0      CONFIG
GigabitEthernet0/1       inside        192.168.0.1       255.255.255.0      CONFIG
GigabitEthernet0/2       dmz1          192.168.1.1       255.255.255.0      CONFIG
GigabitEthernet0/3       dmz2          192.168.2.1       255.255.255.0      CONFIG
Management0/0            mgmt          10.255.0.4        255.255.0.0        CONFIG
```

2. Set up four security levels on the ASA: LAN, DMZ1, DMZ2 and outside. Security levels from high to low: LAN > DMZ1 > DMZ2 > outside.

   Assign security level to each ASA interface. We'll configure four interfaces on the ASA. Their security levels are: inside (100), dmz1(50), dmz2(20) and outside (0).

```
interface GigabitEthernet0/0
 description to WAN
 nameif outside
 security-level 0
 ip address 10.1.1.1 255.255.255.0
!
interface GigabitEthernet0/1
 description to LAN
 nameif inside
 security-level 100
 ip address 192.168.0.1 255.255.255.0
!
interface GigabitEthernet0/2
 description to DMZ1
 nameif dmz1
 security-level 50
```

```
 ip address 192.168.1.1 255.255.255.0
!
interface GigabitEthernet0/3
 description to DMZ2
 nameif dmz2
 security-level 20
 ip address 192.168.2.1 255.255.255.0
```

3. **A Cisco ASA is deployed as an Internet gateway, providing outbound Internet access to all internal hosts.**

    Configure ASA as an Internet gateway and enable Internet access. There are two main tasks to enable internal hosts to go out to the Internet, configuring **Network Address Translation (NAT)** and **route all traffic to the ISP**. You do not need an ACL because all outbound traffic is traversing from higher security level (inside, dmz1 and dmz2) to lower security level (outside). To configure NAT:

    ```
    nat (inside,outside) after-auto source dynamic any interface
    nat (dmz1,outside) after-auto source dynamic any interface
    nat (dmz2,outside) after-auto source dynamic any interface
    ```

    The configuration above states that any traffic coming from inside, dmz1 and dmz2 networks, translate the source IP to the outside interface's IP for outbound Internet traffic. The "after-auto" keyword simply set this NAT the least preferred rule to be evaluated after Manual NAT and Auto NAT are evaluated. The reason we want to give it the least preference is to avoid possible conflict with other NAT rules.

    Since ASA code version 8.3 and later, NAT on the ASA is broken into two types known as Auto NAT (Object NAT) and Manual NAT (Twice NAT). The first of the two, Object NAT, is configured within the definition of a network object.

    The main advantage of Auto NAT is that the ASA automatically orders the rules for processing as to avoid conflicts. This is the easiest form of NAT, but with that ease comes with a limitation in configuration granularity. For example, you cannot make translation decision based on the destination in the packet as you could with the second type of NAT, Manual NAT. Manual NAT is more robust in its granularity, but it requires that the lines be configured in the correct order in order to achieve the correct behavior.

    The other change in NAT is that you either define a NAT or you don't. Traffic that does not match any NAT rules will traverse the firewall without any translation (like NAT exemption but without explicitly configuring it, more like an implicit NAT exemption). The static and global keywords are deprecated. Now it is all about "NAT".

Next is configuring a default gateway and route all traffic to the upstream ISP. 10.1.1.2 is the gateway the ISP provided.

```
route outside 0.0.0.0 0.0.0.0 10.1.1.2
```

Also make sure "inspect icmp" is configured under global_policy. It allows icmp return traffic to pass the ASA while the Ping is initiated from inside hosts.

```
policy-map global_policy
 class inspection_default
  inspect icmp
```

At this point, you should be able to ping the host 10.1.1.200 on the Internet from any internal or DMZ hosts.

```
cisco@LAN-host:~$ ping 10.1.1.200
PING 10.1.1.200 (10.1.1.200) 56(84) bytes of data.
64 bytes from 10.1.1.200: icmp_seq=1 ttl=64 time=5.89 ms
64 bytes from 10.1.1.200: icmp_seq=2 ttl=64 time=3.51 ms
64 bytes from 10.1.1.200: icmp_seq=3 ttl=64 time=2.25 ms
64 bytes from 10.1.1.200: icmp_seq=4 ttl=64 time=2.16 ms
^C
--- 10.1.1.200 ping statistics ---
4 packets transmitted, 4 received, 0% packet loss, time 3004ms
rtt min/avg/max/mdev = 2.165/3.457/5.896/1.506 ms
cisco@LAN-host:~$
cisco@DMZ1-Server:~$ ping 10.1.1.200
PING 10.1.1.200 (10.1.1.200) 56(84) bytes of data.
64 bytes from 10.1.1.200: icmp_seq=1 ttl=64 time=4.88 ms
64 bytes from 10.1.1.200: icmp_seq=2 ttl=64 time=1.40 ms
64 bytes from 10.1.1.200: icmp_seq=3 ttl=64 time=3.61 ms
^C
--- 10.1.1.200 ping statistics ---
3 packets transmitted, 3 received, 0% packet loss, time 2003ms
rtt min/avg/max/mdev = 1.402/3.299/4.880/1.437 ms
cisco@DMZ1-Server:~$
cisco@DMZ2-Server:~$ ping 10.1.1.200
PING 10.1.1.200 (10.1.1.200) 56(84) bytes of data.
64 bytes from 10.1.1.200: icmp_seq=1 ttl=64 time=2.84 ms
64 bytes from 10.1.1.200: icmp_seq=2 ttl=64 time=2.19 ms
64 bytes from 10.1.1.200: icmp_seq=3 ttl=64 time=2.41 ms
^C
--- 10.1.1.200 ping statistics ---
3 packets transmitted, 3 received, 0% packet loss, time 2004ms
rtt min/avg/max/mdev = 2.199/2.484/2.840/0.272 ms
cisco@DMZ2-Server:~$
```

The ASA has been configured to provide outbound Internet access to all internal hosts.

4. Configure static NAT to the web server, grant Internet inbound access to web server.

First, we define two objects for the web server, one for its internal IP and one for its public facing IP.

```
object network WWW-EXT
  host 10.1.1.10
!
object network WWW-INT
  host 192.168.1.10
```

We have two ways of configuring NAT, Auto NAT (Object NAT) and Manual NAT (Twice NAT). For Auto-NAT, insert this configuration under WWW-INT object.

```
nat (dmz1,outside) static WWW-EXT service tcp www www
```

For Manual NAT, define the web service object and configure manual NAT in global configuration mode. In our example, we'll demonstrate Manual NAT. You can only have one set of configurations at a time.

```
object service WEB-SERVICE
  service tcp source eq www
!
nat (dmz1,outside) source static WWW-INT WWW-EXT service WEB-SERVICE WEB-SERVICE
```

When a host matching the IP address 192.168.1.10 on the dmz1 segment establishes a connection sourced from TCP port 80 (WWW) and that connection goes out the outside interface, we want to translate that to be TCP port 80 (WWW) on the outside interface and translate that IP address to be 10.1.1.10.

That seems a little odd… "sourced from TCP port 80 (www)", but web traffic is destined to port 80. It is important to understand that these NAT rules are bi-directional in nature. As a result, you can re-phrase this sentence by flipping the wording around. The result makes a lot more sense:

When hosts on the outside establish a connection to 10.1.1.10 on destination TCP port 80 (www), we will translate the destination IP address to 192.168.1.10 and the destination port will be TCP port 80 (www) and send it out the dmz1.

Because traffic from the outside to the dmz1 network is denied by the ASA by default, users on the Internet cannot reach the web server despite the NAT configuration. We will need to configure ACLs and allow Internet inbound traffic to access the web server.

```
access-list OUTSIDE extended permit tcp any object WWW-INT eq www
!
access-group OUTSIDE in interface outside
```

The ACL states, permit traffic from anywhere to the web server (WWW-INT: 192.168.1.10) on port 80. The ASA is configured to allow inbound web traffic to go to the web server.

5. Enforce inter-security segment access control

Let's recap the default behavior on a Cisco ASA.
- Traffic initiated from a lower security interface is denied when going to a higher security interface
- Traffic initiated from a higher security interface is allowed when going to a lower security interface

In our lab specifically,
- Traffic initiated from "inside" is allowed to go to any other interface segments – "dmz1", "dmz2" and "outside".
- Traffic initiated from "dmz1" is allowed to go to "dmz2" and "outside". It is denied when going to "inside".
- Traffic initiated from "dmz2" is allowed only when going to "outside". All other segment access is denied.

The default rules can be overwritten by ACLs. In our example, we need the guests in dmz2 to be able to use the DNS servers in dmz1. We'll need to configure ACLs to specifically allow the access.

```
! define network objects
object network INSIDE-NET
 subnet 192.168.0.0 255.255.255.0
!
object network DMZ1-NET
 subnet 192.168.1.0 255.255.255.0
!
! define DNS server object
object network DNS-SERVER
 host 192.168.1.10
!
access-list DMZ2-ACL extended permit udp any object DNS-SERVER eq domain
access-list DMZ2-ACL extended deny ip any object INSIDE-NET
access-list DMZ2-ACL extended deny ip any object DMZ1-NET
```

```
access-list DMZ2-ACL extended permit ip any any
!
access-group DMZ2-ACL in interface dmz2
```

The ACLs allow traffic initiated from dmz2 to access the DNS server on UDP port 53. Remember there is an implicit "deny ip any any" at the end of the ACL. If we stopped here dmz2's Internet access will be broken. We added three more lines to deny access to dmz1 and inside networks while allowing the reset of traffic to go to the Internet. What about ACLs on dmz1 and inside interfaces? We do not need any ACLs on those interfaces because the default security behavior meets our requirements.

It has satisfied all the requirements.

6. **Finally make sure you have a fully working network, with no errors or warnings in "show logging" on the ASA.**

   A few validation and troubleshooting techniques will be demonstrated to quickly identify and troubleshoot problem if any.

   The first technique is using ICMP debug to verify network connectivity. Obviously, ping is working does not conclude everything else is also working. However, it is a simple tool to confirm that packet from point A can reach point B. In our example we wanted to verify that hosts in each subnet of inside, dmz1 and dmz2 have Internet access. We tried pinging the Internet host at 10.1.1.200 from each internal network.

   On the ASA, we enabled ICMP debug mode and made the terminal as the debug message output monitor. By default, the debug messages are sent to the log buffer instead of the screen. You need to view the logs by doing "show logging". In our case, we wanted to see the logs immediately as they are popping up on the screen.

```
ASA1# debug icmp trace
ASA1# terminal monitor
```

Ping was initiated from inside host 192.168.0.200, dmz1 host 192.168.1.10 and dmz2 host 192.168.2.10. Responses are being received.

```
ASA1# ICMP echo request from inside:192.168.0.200 to outside:10.1.1.200 ID=2357 seq=1 len=56
ICMP echo request translating inside:192.168.0.200 to outside:10.1.1.1
ICMP echo reply from outside:10.1.1.200 to inside:10.1.1.1 ID=2357 seq=1 len=56
ICMP echo reply untranslating outside:10.1.1.1 to inside:192.168.0.200

ASA1# ICMP echo request from dmz1:192.168.1.10 to outside:10.1.1.200 ID=2485 seq=1 len=56
ICMP echo request translating dmz1:192.168.1.10 to outside:10.1.1.1
ICMP echo reply from outside:10.1.1.200 to dmz1:10.1.1.1 ID=2485 seq=1 len=56
ICMP echo reply untranslating outside:10.1.1.1 to dmz1:192.168.1.10

ASA1# ICMP echo request from dmz2:192.168.2.10 to outside:10.1.1.200 ID=2353 seq=1 len=56
ICMP echo request translating dmz2:192.168.2.10 to outside:10.1.1.1
ICMP echo reply from outside:10.1.1.200 to dmz2:10.1.1.1 ID=2353 seq=1 len=56
ICMP echo reply untranslating outside:10.1.1.1 to dmz2:192.168.2.10

ASA1#
```

Study the debug message and you'll see exactly how ICMP packets flow through the network.

1. ICMP echo request from inside:192.168.0.200 to outside:10.1.1.200 (The ASA sees an incoming ping packet from inside interface host 192.168.0.200 and trying to reach host 10.1.1.200 on the outside interface)
2. ICMP echo request translating inside:192.168.0.200 to outside:10.1.1.1 (The ASA detected a NAT rule would match and used it to translate the source IP from 192.168.0.200 to 10.1.1.1)
3. ICMP echo reply from outside:10.1.1.200 to inside:10.1.1.1 (The host 10.1.1.200 on the Internet replied to the ping request and send the return traffic to 10.1.1.1)
4. ICMP echo reply un-translating outside:10.1.1.1 to inside:192.168.0.200 (The ASA sees the ping return traffic and it matches an established traffic session when the outbound ping traffic was generated. The ASA knows exactly who requested it and who is desperately waiting for it. The ASA un-translate the IP from 10.1.1.1 to 192.168.0.200 and send it to 192.168.0.200).

After testing, do remember to deactivate the debug mode because it is system resource consuming.

```
ASA1# no debug all
```

The second technique is using Packet Tracer to simulate packets going through the ASA and see how the ASA treats the packet step-by-step. It is an excellent tool when you do not have access to either side of the servers to generate real traffic. Or before going live, you wanted to make sure the configuration will do what's intended. We'll do two packet tracer tests to validate these critical services:

- The ASA allows inbound web traffic to the web server in DMZ1.
- The ASA allows users in DMZ2 to access the DNS server in DMZ1.

We first simulate web browsing traffic initiated from a host on the internet with IP 10.1.1.200, trying to reach the web server on port 80. The following command sates:

"Generate a fake packet and push it through to the ASA's outside interface in the inbound direction. The packet comes with source IP 10.1.1.200 using a random high port number 1234 and destination IP 10.1.1.10 to the web server on port 80."

```
ASA1# packet-tracer input outside tcp 10.1.1.200 1234 10.1.1.10 http detailed
Phase: 1
Type: ACCESS-LIST
Subtype:
Result: ALLOW
Config:
Implicit Rule
Additional Information:
 Forward Flow based lookup yields rule:
 in  id=0x7fffd1991830, priority=1, domain=permit, deny=false
        hits=43, user_data=0x0, cs_id=0x0, l3_type=0x8
        src mac=0000.0000.0000, mask=0000.0000.0000
        dst mac=0000.0000.0000, mask=0100.0000.0000
        input_ifc=outside, output_ifc=any

Phase: 2
Type: UN-NAT
Subtype: static
Result: ALLOW
Config:
nat (dmz1,outside) source static WWW-INT WWW-EXT service WEB-SERVICE WEB-SERVICE
Additional Information:
NAT divert to egress interface dmz1
Untranslate 10.1.1.10/80 to 192.168.1.200/80

Phase: 3
Type: ACCESS-LIST
Subtype: log
Result: ALLOW
Config:
access-group OUTSIDE in interface outside
access-list OUTSIDE extended permit tcp any object WWW-INT eq www
Additional Information:
 Forward Flow based lookup yields rule:
 in  id=0x7fffd12e7660, priority=13, domain=permit, deny=false
        hits=1, user_data=0x7fffd8eb9d00, cs_id=0x0, use_real_addr, flags=0x0, protocol=6
        src ip/id=0.0.0.0, mask=0.0.0.0, port=0, tag=any
        dst ip/id=192.168.1.200, mask=255.255.255.255, port=80, tag=any,
dscp=0x0
        input_ifc=outside, output_ifc=any
```

```
Phase: 4
Type: NAT
Subtype:
Result: ALLOW
Config:
nat (dmz1,outside) source static WWW-INT WWW-EXT service WEB-SERVICE
WEB-SERVICE
Additional Information:
Static translate 10.1.1.200/1234 to 10.1.1.200/1234
 Forward Flow based lookup yields rule:
 in  id=0x7fffd1cc1b50, priority=6, domain=nat, deny=false
        hits=1, user_data=0x7fffd12e6270, cs_id=0x0, flags=0x0, protocol=6
        src ip/id=0.0.0.0, mask=0.0.0.0, port=0, tag=any
        dst ip/id=10.1.1.10, mask=255.255.255.255, port=80, tag=any, dscp=0x0
        input_ifc=outside, output_ifc=dmz1
...
output omitted for brevity
...
Result:
input-interface: outside
input-status: up
input-line-status: up
output-interface: dmz1
output-status: up
output-line-status: up
Action: allow
```

Looking through the packet tracer results, we learned the following:

1. Phase 1 is Layer 2 MAC level ACL, we do not have any MAC level restriction configured and all traffic is allowed by default.
2. At Phase 2, packet is being un-NAT'd before sending to the outside interface ACL. That's why we needed to use the real-IP or the internal IP WWW-INT when configuring the ACL. It is a major change since ASA code 8.3. Prior to code 8.3, ACL was checked first before un-NAT'ing.
3. Phase 3 shows the outside ACL is being verified and the traffic is allowed.
4. The reset of the phases put the packet through various of policy checks such as QoS, policy-maps and etc. We don't have any of those configured so there was no effect to the packet.
5. In the end, a nice summary is displayed. The input interface is outside, the output interface is dmz1 and the traffic is sent through successfully.

Similarly, we can do the pack tracer testing between dmz2 and dmz1, to verify the host in dmz2 has access to dmz1's DNS server.

```
ASA1# packet-tracer input dmz2 udp 192.168.2.10 1234 192.168.1.10 domain detailed
Phase: 1
Type: ACCESS-LIST
Subtype:
Result: ALLOW
Config:
Implicit Rule
Additional Information:
 Forward Flow based lookup yields rule:
 in  id=0x7fffd1a76710, priority=1, domain=permit, deny=false
        hits=12, user_data=0x0, cs_id=0x0, l3_type=0x8
        src mac=0000.0000.0000, mask=0000.0000.0000
        dst mac=0000.0000.0000, mask=0100.0000.0000
        input_ifc=dmz2, output_ifc=any

Phase: 2
Type: ROUTE-LOOKUP
Subtype: Resolve Egress Interface
Result: ALLOW
Config:
Additional Information:
found next-hop 192.168.1.10 using egress ifc  dmz1

Phase: 3
Type: ACCESS-LIST
Subtype: log
Result: ALLOW
Config:
access-group DMZ2-ACL in interface dmz2
access-list DMZ2-ACL extended permit udp any object DNS-SERVER eq domain
Additional Information:
 Forward Flow based lookup yields rule:
 in  id=0x7fffd1cdad10, priority=13, domain=permit, deny=false
        hits=0, user_data=0x7fffd8eb9b80, cs_id=0x0, use_real_addr, flags=0x0, protocol=17
        src ip/id=0.0.0.0, mask=0.0.0.0, port=0, tag=any
        dst ip/id=192.168.1.10, mask=255.255.255.255, port=53, tag=any, dscp=0x0
        input_ifc=dmz2, output_ifc=any
...
output omitted for brevity
...
```

```
Result:
input-interface: dmz2
input-status: up
input-line-status: up
output-interface: dmz1
output-status: up
output-line-status: up
Action: allow
```

Since there is no NAT involved, Phase 2 went straight to route lookup. The output interface dmz1 was identified. Phase 3 checks the ACL, and it granted traffic to go through. The reset of the phases stayed the same. In the end, the packet was sent through dmz1 interface successfully.

Both packet tracer results confirmed our configuration is correct. Let's try packet tracer testing on something that is not supposed to work. We wanted to see the ASA actually blocks the traffic.

The web server is not configured to serve FTP traffic. We'll send an FTP request to the webs server and see what happens.

```
ASA1# packet-tracer input outside tcp 10.1.1.200 1234 10.1.1.10 ftp detailed
Phase: 1
Type: ROUTE-LOOKUP
Subtype: Resolve Egress Interface
Result: ALLOW
Config:
Additional Information:
found next-hop 10.1.1.10 using egress ifc  outside

Result:
input-interface: outside
input-status: up
input-line-status: up
output-interface: outside
output-status: up
output-line-status: up
Action: drop
Drop-reason: (nat-no-xlate-to-pat-pool) Connection to PAT address without pre-existing xlate
```

The ASA dropped the packet because there are no NAT rules configured to transfer FTP traffic to anything. It didn't even get to the ACL check point.

All requirements have been completed and verified. Let's move on to the next lab.

Topology 6: Configuring L2TP Over IPSec VPN on Cisco ASA (Security)

Overview

L2TP is a combination of PPTP and Layer 2 Forwarding (L2F), a technology developed by Cisco. L2TP combines the best features of PPTP and L2F. Even the underlying tunneling technology still utilizes PPP specifications. the encryption is done by IPSec in transport mode. L2TP/IPSec protocol uses UDP port 500.

Encapsulation

L2TP has two layers of encapsulations – inner L2TP encapsulation and outer layer IPSec encapsulation. The inner layer comprised of an L2TP header and a UDP header wrapped around the PPP frame. The outer layer adds IPSec ESP (Encapsulating Security Payload) header and trailer to the first layer. The IPSec authentication trailer provides message integrity check and authentication.

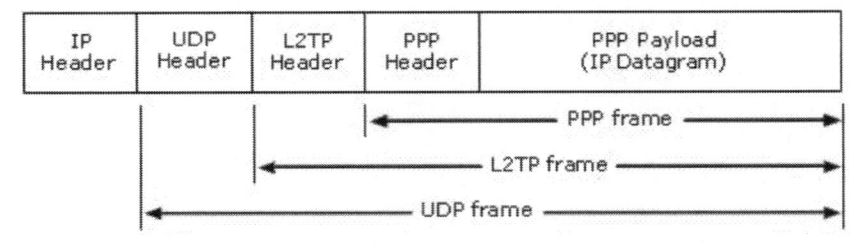

IP Header	UDP Header	L2TP Header	PPP Header	PPP Payload (IP Datagram)

                                     ←———— PPP frame ————→
                      ←———————— L2TP frame ————————→
        ←———————————— UDP frame ————————————→

Encryption

Data encryption is done with one of the following protocols by using encryption keys generated from the IKE negotiation process. AES-256 (Advanced Encryption Standard), AES-192, AES-128, and 3DES encryption algorithms. Since vulnerabilities have been found in 3DES algorithms, using 3DES is no longer recommended.

Benefits

Unlike PPTP and SSTP, L2TP/IPsec enables machine authentication at the IPsec layer and user level authentication at the PPP layer. It supports either computer certificates or a pre-shared key as the authentication method for IPsec. L2TP/IPsec provides data confidentiality, data integrity, and data authentication

Furthermore, L2TP/IPSec supports the highest encryption. It checks data integrity and encapsulates the data twice. It is not the fastest VPN solution because of the double encapsulation overhead but you can't really notice it running on the modem hardware.

Network Topology

A simple network is composed of a Corp LAN, a Cisco ASA acting as an Internet gateway and firewall. Remote VPN users connect to the Corp LAN using L2TP/IPSec VPN. A DHCP pool is reserved on the ASA for VPN users. We'll also implement "split tunneling" so that regular Internet traffic is not sent through the tunnel. For simplicity, VPN user authentication is done locally on the ASA. You can configure RADIUS authentication to an AD. It is outside the scope of this article.

- Corp LAN: 172.30.30.0/24
- DHCP Pool for VPN users: 192.168.199.100 – 200

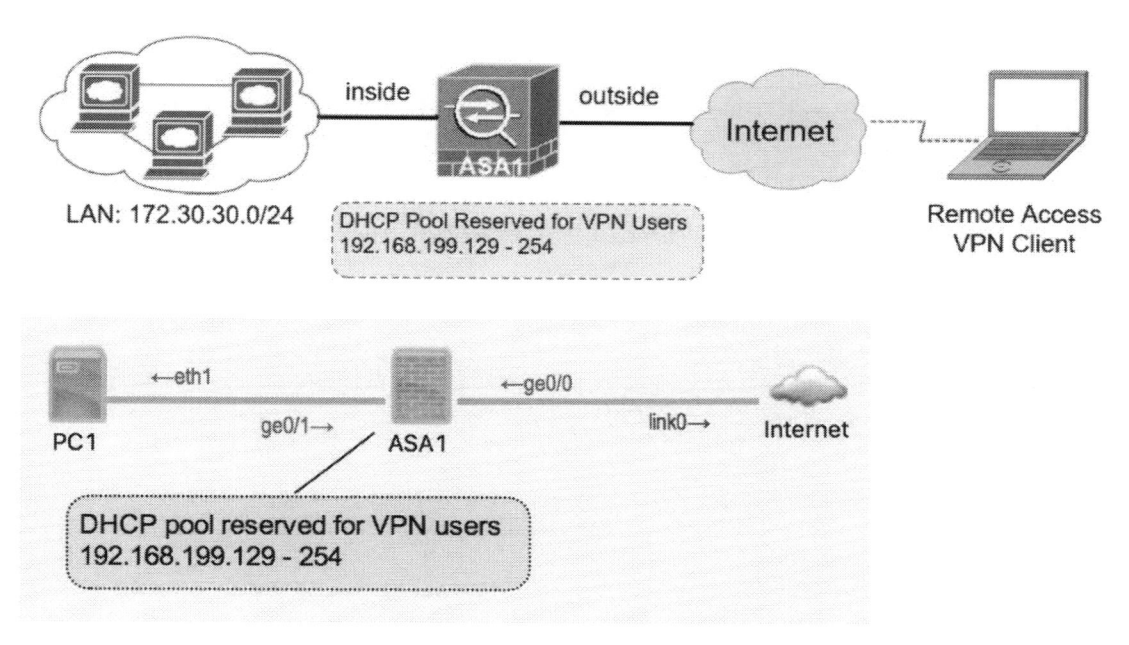

The network topology includes one Cisco ASA and one Linux server.

What has been done in the initial configuration:

- Wiring among the switches and routers
- Host names, ASA and server IPs and default gateway
- OOB management IP addresses
- Credentials
    - Server username / password: cisco / cisco
    - ASA enable password: cisco
    - Group password: MyVPNPassWord!
    - VPN username / password: vpnuser / PASS123

Requirements

1. Configure DHCP pool (192.168.199.129 - 254) for VPN users.

2. Configure group-policy and tunnel-group.
3. Implement "split tunneling" so that regular Internet traffic is not sent through the tunnel.
4. VPN user authentication is done locally on the ASA.

Solutions

0. Verify initial configuration and basic network connectivity.

The Linux server was assigned with IP 172.30.30.10/24 and default gateway pointing to the ASA (172.30.30.1) using its eth1 interface. (this step has been done for you. Review initial.virl file)

```
#!/bin/sh
 ifconfig eth1 up 172.30.30.10 netmask 255.255.255.0
 route add -net 0.0.0.0 netmask 0.0.0.0 gw 172.30.30.1 dev eth1
exit 0
```

Login the Linux server and issue the following commands to verify network connectivity:

```
cisco@PC1:~$ ifconfig eth1
cisco@PC1:~$ netstat -rn
cisco@PC1:~$ ping 172.30.30.1 ! make sure it can ping the ASA
```

You should get results similar to this.

```
cisco@PC1:~$ ifconfig eth1
eth1    Link encap:Ethernet  HWaddr fa:16:3e:77:22:be
        inet addr:172.30.30.10  Bcast:172.30.30.255  Mask:255.255.255.0
        inet6 addr: fe80::f816:3eff:fe77:22be/64 Scope:Link
        UP BROADCAST RUNNING MULTICAST  MTU:1500  Metric:1
        RX packets:4 errors:0 dropped:0 overruns:0 frame:0
        TX packets:10 errors:0 dropped:0 overruns:0 carrier:0
        collisions:0 txqueuelen:1000
        RX bytes:316 (316.0 B)  TX bytes:788 (788.0 B)

cisco@PC1:~$ netstat -rn
Kernel IP routing table
Destination     Gateway         Genmask         Flags   MSS Window  irtt Iface
0.0.0.0         172.30.30.1     0.0.0.0         UG      0 0          0 eth1
0.0.0.0         10.255.0.1      0.0.0.0         UG      0 0          0 eth0
10.255.0.0      0.0.0.0         255.255.0.0     U       0 0          0 eth0
169.254.169.254 10.255.0.1      255.255.255.255 UGH     0 0          0 eth0
172.30.30.0     0.0.0.0         255.255.255.0   U       0 0          0 eth1
cisco@PC1:~$ ping 172.30.30.1
PING 172.30.30.1 (172.30.30.1) 56(84) bytes of data.
64 bytes from 172.30.30.1: icmp_seq=1 ttl=255 time=1.36 ms
64 bytes from 172.30.30.1: icmp_seq=2 ttl=255 time=1.49 ms
64 bytes from 172.30.30.1: icmp_seq=3 ttl=255 time=1.29 ms
^C
--- 172.30.30.1 ping statistics ---
3 packets transmitted, 3 received, 0% packet loss, time 2003ms
rtt min/avg/max/mdev = 1.295/1.385/1.493/0.092 ms
cisco@PC1:~$
```

Login ASA1 and verify the IP addresses on the interfaces. And the ASA can ping the Linux server on 172.30.30.10.

```
ASA1# show ip
System IP Addresses:
Interface              Name        IP address      Subnet mask     Method
GigabitEthernet0/0     outside     172.16.1.78     255.255.255.0   CONFIG
GigabitEthernet0/1     inside      172.30.30.1     255.255.255.0   CONFIG
Management0/0          mgmt        10.255.0.11     255.255.0.0     CONFIG
Current IP Addresses:
Interface              Name        IP address      Subnet mask     Method
GigabitEthernet0/0     outside     172.16.1.78     255.255.255.0   CONFIG
GigabitEthernet0/1     inside      172.30.30.1     255.255.255.0   CONFIG
Management0/0          mgmt        10.255.0.11     255.255.0.0     CONFIG
ASA1#
ASA1#
```

```
ASA1# ping 172.30.30.10
Type escape sequence to abort.
Sending 5, 100-byte ICMP Echos to 172.30.30.10, timeout is 2 seconds:
!!!!!
Success rate is 100 percent (5/5), round-trip min/avg/max = 1/1/1 ms
ASA1#
```

We have verified the basic network connectivity and are ready to move on to the tasks.

1. Configure DHCP pool (192.168.199.129 - 254) for VPN users.

The VNP user DHCP pool should not overlap with your existing network. It is not a good idea to share a portion of your existing LAN subnet with VPN users. If you put them on the same network, they would have access to everything on the same subnet. For better security and flexible traffic control, I would put VPN users on their own subnet, and in a range that can be expressed by a subnet mask. For example, 192.168.199.129 – 254 /25 (subnet mask 255.255.255.128). The benefit of doing so is that you can do route summarization, ACL to cover this subnet easily and cleanly. Any security policies can be applied to the VPN user subnet without having to share with other subnets.

```
ip local pool VPNPOOL 192.168.199.129-192.168.199.254 mask
255.255.255.128
```

2. Configure group-policy and tunnel-group.

First step, we need to create **group-policy and tunnel-group**. Note that I use all capital letters for variables being referenced in the command. They are just a name, you can name them anything make sense in your environment.

```
group-policy SSLGROUPPOLICY internal
group-policy SSLGROUPPOLICY attributes
dns-server value 4.2.2.2 ! DNS servers
vpn-tunnel-protocol l2tp-ipsec ! specifying the protocol being used
default-domain value speaknetworks.com
intercept-dhcp enable
```

Next we define a "Tunnel Group" for the tunnel, You MUST use the default group with default name "DefaultRAGroup"(the only exception is if you use certificate based authentication).

```
tunnel-group DefaultRAGroup general-attributes
address-pool VPNPOOL !VPN user will be assigned with an IP in the pool
default-group-policy SSLGROUPPOLICY !references group-policy defined
earlier
authentication-server-group LOCAL !user local authentication
!
tunnel-group DefaultRAGroup ppp-attributes
no authentication pap
authentication chap
authentication ms-chap-v1
authentication ms-chap-v2

tunnel-group DefaultRAGroup ipsec-attributes
Ikev1 pre-shared-key MyVPNPassWord ! group password for all VPN users
```

Configure VPN Phase 1 and Phase 2

Although some the configuration blocks will appear in the ASA's "show run" configuration before others, we'll configuration it by following a more logical order of workflow- define a parameter, reference it in a modular configuration, apply the modular to global configuration.

First, we define transform-set used in Phase 2. In this lab, we use 3DES encryption and SHA hashing. The tunnel will be in transport mode instead of VPN mode (default).

```
crypto ipsec ikev1 transform-set ESP-3DES-SHA esp-3des esp-sha-hmac
crypto ipsec ikev1 transform-set ESP-3DES-SHA mode transport
```

Next, we prepare for Phase 2 configuration. We configure a "dynamic-map" to use the transform-set defined above. Then setup a crypto map, referencing the dynamic-map, and assign it to the outside interface of the ASA. The outside interface is Internet facing where VPN users come in from. The numbers 10 and 20 are arbitrary sequential numbers to differentiate one crypto map / VPN tunnels from another. You can have multiple VPN tunnels terminated on a single ASA.

```
crypto dynamic-map L2TP-MAP 10 set ikev1 transform-set ESP-3DES-SHA
crypto map L2TPVPN 20 ipsec-isakmp dynamic L2TP-MAP
crypto map L2TPVPN interface outside
```

Phase 1 configuration is followed. We create a Phase 1 policy, which defines using pre-share key for authentication, SHA for hashing and Diffie Hellman group 2 for secure key exchange. The number "10" is a sequential number that the ASA checks in that order. If you want a policy to be evaluated first, make a smaller number. Finally, we enable the IKE on the outside interface.

```
crypto ikev1 policy 10
 authentication pre-share
 encryption 3des
 hash sha
 group 2
 lifetime 86400
!
crypto ikev1 enable outside
```

We have finished all VPN related configuration.

3. Implement "split tunneling" so that regular Internet traffic is not sent through the tunnel.

By default, all traffic is sent through the VPN tunnel once a client is connected. Even though it is the most secure way to manage VPN users (i.e. centralized web content filtering), in a lot of instances people prefer splitting the Internet traffic off the VPN tunnel to save Internet bandwidth on the VPN headend such as a Corp network.

Configure a standard ACL to cover Corp LAN

```
access-list Split-Tunnel-ACL standard permit 172.30.30.0 255.255.255.0
```

Configure NAT exclusion between Corp LAN and VPN users

```
object network Corp-Subnet
 subnet 172.30.30.0 255.255.255.0
!
object network L2TP-Subnet
 subnet 192.168.199.128 255.255.255.128
!
nat (inside,outside) source static Corp-Subnet Corp-Subnet destination static L2TP-Subnet L2TP-Subnet no-proxy-arp route-lookup
```

Add Split-Tunneling configuration to the group-policy

```
group-policy SSLGROUPPOLICY attributes
 split-tunnel-policy tunnelspecified
 split-tunnel-network-list value Split-Tunnel-ACL
```

User can't connect without a way to authenticate. We'll use local user accounts configured on the ASA.

4. VPN user authentication is done locally on the ASA.

Don't overlook the keyword "mschap" in the end when you are creating user accounts on the ASA. Without it, users would not be able to connect to the VPN.

```
username vpnuser password PASS123 mschap
```

You have completed configuring L2TP over IPSec VPN on Cisco ASA lab. You can try configuring the Linux server to act as VPN client and connect to the ASA. It is outside the scope of this workbook.

Troubleshooting Common Issues

The most common issues that I have seen many people ran into including myself. I thought it is a good idea to document them here for your reference.

Issue 1: Authentication failed

You must configure a local username account with "mschap" keyword. If you didn't add the mschap keyword in the end when creating a user account, you get this error in logs. ASA complains about no username identified. The ASA only uses the accounts with mschap option enabled.

```
May 12 2018 11:28:49: %ASA-4-113019: Group = DefaultRAGroup, Username = , IP = 123.52.159.6, Session disconnected. Session Type: IPsecOverNatT, Duration: 0h:00m:03s, Bytes xmt: 3468, Bytes rcv: 3090, Reason: L2TP initiated
```

```
ASA1# config t
ASA1(config)# username vpnuser password PASS123 ?

configure mode commands/options:
  attributes     Enter the attributes sub-command mode for the specified user
  encrypted      Indicates the <password> entered is encrypted
  mschap         The password will be converted to unicode and hashed using MD4.
                   User entries must be created this way if they are to be
                   authenticated using MSCHAPv1 or MSCHAPv2
  nt-encrypted   Indicates the <password> entered has been converted to unicode
                   and hashed using MD4, and can be used for MS-CHAP.
  pbkdf2         Indicates that the <password> entered has been salted and
                   hashed using the pbkdf2 key derivation algorithm
  privilege      Enter the privilege level for this user
  <cr>
ASA1(config)# username vpnuser password PASS123 mschap ?

configure mode commands/options:
  attributes   Enter the attributes sub-command mode for the specified user
  privilege    Enter the privilege level for this user
  <cr>
ASA1(config)# exit
ASA1# sho run | i username
username vpnuser password tVwP2tvXdJ1aoRMBIoF7TA== nt-encrypted
username cisco password 3USUcOPFUiMC04Jk encrypted privilege 15
ASA1#
```

Issue 2: Tunnel-group issue

You *have to* use the default tunnel-group named *DefaultRAGroup*. If you used any other tunnel group names, you'll get error in the logs.

```
%ASA-4-713903: Group = 166.52.19.6, IP = 166.52.19.6, Can't find a valid tunnel group, aborting...!
%ASA-4-713903: IP = 166.52.19.6, Header invalid, missing SA payload! (next payload = 4)
%ASA-4-713903: IP = 166.52.19.6, Header invalid, missing SA payload! (next payload = 4)
```

Issue 3: Connected to VPN but unable to access Corp LAN hosts

After the VPN is connected, you found that the ASA inside interface is the only IP you can ping (assuming icmp is allowed on ASA). And errors show in the logs:

```
%ASA-5-305013: Asymmetric NAT rules matched for forward and reverse flows; Connection for icmp src outside:192.168.199.129 dst inside:172.30.30.30 (type 8, code 0) denied due to NAT reverse path failure
```

The most common cause of this error is NAT exemption. Make sure you have "nonat" configured in the pre-8.3 code and "nat (inside,outside)" statement configured in post-8.3 code.

Still having issue? Use packet-tracer to verify traffic flow

```
ASA# packet-tracer input outside icmp 192.168.199.100 8 0 172.30.30.30

Phase: 1
Type: ROUTE-LOOKUP
Subtype: input
Result: ALLOW
Config:
Additional Information:
in 172.30.30.0 255.255.255.0 inside

Phase: 2
Type: ACCESS-LIST
Subtype: log
Result: ALLOW
Config:
access-group outside_access_inside in interface outside
access-list outside_access_inside extended permit icmp any any

Additional Information:

Phase: 3
Type: IP-OPTIONS
Subtype:
Result: ALLOW
Config:
Additional Information:

Phase: 4
Type: CP-PUNT
Subtype:
Result: ALLOW
```

Config:
Additional Information:

Phase: 5
Type: L2TP-PPP
Subtype:
Result: ALLOW
Config:
Additional Information:

Phase: 6
Type: INSPECT
Subtype: np-inspect
Result: ALLOW
Config:
Additional Information:

Phase: 7
Type:
Subtype:
Result: ALLOW
Config:
Additional Information:

Phase: 8
Type: VPN
Subtype: ipsec-tunnel-flow
Result: ALLOW
Config:
Additional Information:

Phase: 9
Type: DEBUG-ICMP
Subtype:
Result: ALLOW
Config:
Additional Information:

Phase: 10
Type: NAT-EXEMPT
Subtype: rpf-check
Result: ALLOW
Config:
Additional Information:

Phase: 11
Type: NAT
Subtype: rpf-check

```
Result: ALLOW
Config:
nat (inside) 1 172.30.30.0 255.255.255.0
match ip inside 172.30.30.0 255.255.255.0 outside any dynamic
translation to pool 1 (76.176.134.86 [Interface PAT])
translate_hits = 623987, untranslate_hits = 96153
Additional Information:

Phase: 12
Type: FLOW-CREATION
Subtype:
Result: ALLOW
Config:
Additional Information:
New flow created with id 1700646, packet dispatched to next module
Result:
input-interface: outside
input-status: up
input-line-status: up
output-interface: inside
output-status: up
output-line-status: up
Action: allow
```

If you did not have "NAT exemption" configured, you'll get DROP in Phase 10:

```
Phase: 10
Type: NAT
Subtype: rpf-check
Result: DROP
Config:
nat (inside) 1 172.30.30.0 255.255.255.0
match ip inside 172.30.30.0 255.255.255.0 outside any
dynamic translation to pool 1 (76.176.134.86 [Interface PAT])
translate_hits = 623719, untranslate_hits = 96134
```

Topology 7: Configuring Automatic ISP Failover (WAN, BGP)

Overview

As the internet bandwidth becomes cheaper, organizations have upgraded their primary circuits to higher capacity circuits with lower cost. Some chose to keep their legacy service provider as a backup circuit. BGP is enabled on the Customer Edge (CE) routers to provide redundancy and load balancing. However, given the nature of BGP is a path or distance vector routing protocol, it does not take bandwidth and circuit costs into consideration when making routing decisions. The question comes how we can design a network so that the circuits with higher capacity and cheaper costs are utilized first. We keep the lower bandwidth or/and higher cost circuit as an "active" backup without losing the automatic failover provided by BGP. In this lab, we'll cover automatic ISP failover over uneven bandwidth circuits using HSRP, IP SLA and BGP technologies.

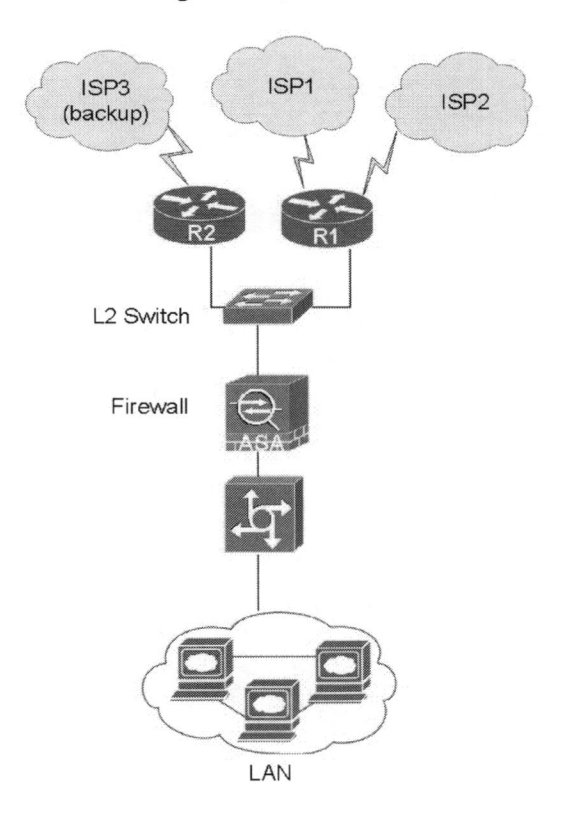

- A network is comprised of three ISPs and two WAN routers R1 and R2.
- Two high capacity Internet circuits from two ISPs are terminated on R1. We use them as primary circuit.

- A lower capacity, high cost Internet circuit is terminated on R2. We only want to use it when both primary ISPs are down.
- WAN circuits failover and fail back should happen in automated fashion.

Network Topology

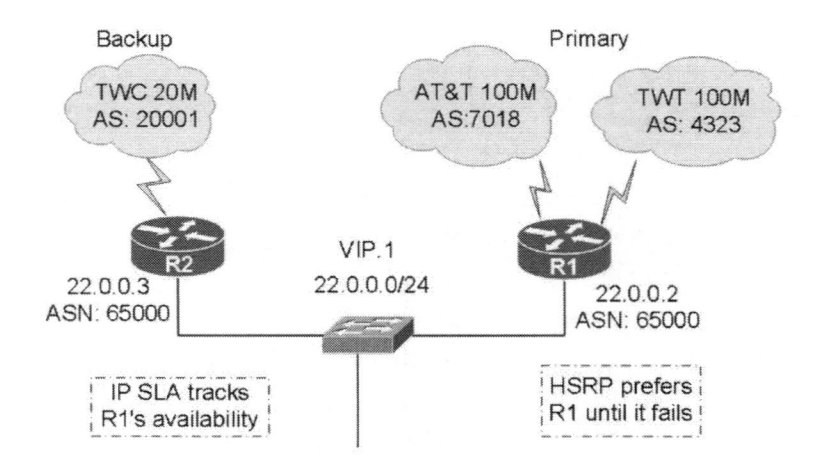

Design Principles

If there was only R1 with two ISPs, the design is rather simple. With the consideration of R2 and its backup ISP, we need to make sure the network is aware of its existence and automatically shifts traffic to R2 when R1 fails.

The first step is to establish basic BGP connectivity on all three WAN routers with their upstream ISPs. Since we are not a service provider providing Internet transit, and we want to conserve router resources, we'll configure the WAN routers only to receive ISP's directly connected prefixes and default route. Because the circuits on R1 have much higher bandwidth capacity, we want to use them for all outbound and inbound traffic. Let's break down the "outbound" and "inbound" into two separate discussions.

Outbound traffic:

For outbound traffic, as long as the WAN router has a default route pointing to its upstream provider, user traffic can be forwarded to the Internet. In our case, three WAN routers each learn a default route from their upstream provider. R1 is preferred over R2 to act as the Internet gateway for internal users. This is done by configuring Hot Standby Routing Protocol (HSRP). A VIP is configured with R1 acting as the live gateway. R2 keeps track of R1's availability, and it takes over R1's role as soon as R1 is detected down.

Inbound traffic:

When BGP announces our prefix (22.0.0.0/24) to the Internet over multiple ISPs, it is known by other ISPs that there are more than one ways to reach us. This is where the distance-vector BGP routing protocol comes to play. When a user on the Internet wants to reach us, the user's ISP looks at its routing table and figure out the best and shortest path to connect to our WAN routers. There are many BGP attributes to be considered when making routing decisions. For now, you can think of the shortest path to reach us is the best route to be chosen. What if we don't want ISP3, the TWC backup circuit to be ever chosen unless it is the only option? There are several techniques we can use to "influence" the Internet to less prefer using ISP3 to reach us. Please note the word "influence". There is no guarantee that the ISP will not be chosen. The technique includes prepending AS numbers, using BGP community to advise your upstream provider to less prefer the prefix you announced to them and etc. But they all come with some caveats. Prepending AS numbers works in some cases but it never worked well in real world because AS Path is not the only attribute the Internet transit ISPs evaluate when making routing decisions. Using BGP community to advise your upstream ISP can only affect your directly connected ISP and its peering ISPs. Many times, it is a manual process when you have to change the community or withdraw the announcement.

Our design concept works as following: R2 does not announce our prefix until R1 is declared down. We use IP SLA to track the availability of R1 and tell BGP to begin announcing the prefix in case R1 becomes unavailable. In this design, we have full control of when the backup ISP3 is being activated.

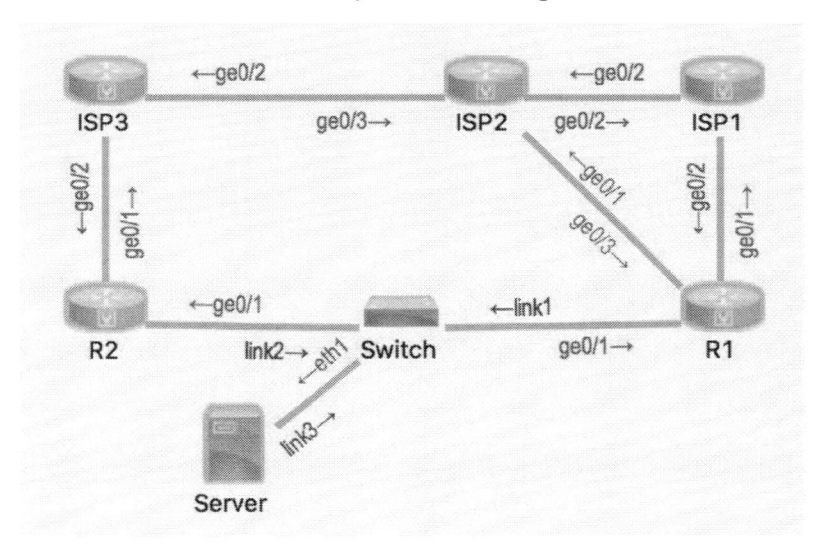

The network topology includes one switch, five routers and a Linux server. The Linux server is used to mimic end user's PC. It can be used to perform Ping and Traceroute testing.

What has been done in the initial configuration:

- Wiring among the switches and routers
- Host names and basic IP address on interfaces
- OOB management IP addresses

- Username / Password for server and routers: cisco / cisco

Requirements

1. A network is comprised of three ISPs and two WAN routers R1 and R2.
2. Two high capacity Internet circuits from two ISPs are terminated on R1. We use them as the primary circuit.
3. A lower capacity, high cost Internet circuit is terminated on R2. We shall use it only when both primary ISPs are down.
4. WAN circuits failover and fail back should happen in automated fashion.

Solutions

1. Establish eBGP peering with upstream service providers on each WAN router.

On R1 we are peering with AT&T (ASN7018) TWT (ASN4323). And on R2 we are peering with TWC (ASN20001).

```
! R1
router bgp 65000
 no synchronization
 bgp log-neighbor-changes
 network 22.0.0.0 mask 255.255.255.0
 neighbor 12.12.12.1 remote-as 7018
 neighbor 12.12.12.1 description ATT
 neighbor 12.12.12.1 soft-reconfiguration inbound
 neighbor 12.12.12.1 prefix-list ATT-7018-OUT-FILTER out
 neighbor 12.12.12.1 prefix-list ATT-7018-IN-FILTER in
 neighbor 12.12.12.1 route-map ATT-7018-INBOUND in
 neighbor 12.12.12.1 maximum-prefix 600000 95 warning-only
!
 neighbor 206.206.206.1 remote-as 4323
 neighbor 206.206.206.1 description TWT
 neighbor 206.206.206.1 soft-reconfiguration inbound
 neighbor 206.206.206.1 prefix-list TWT-4323-OUT-FILTER out
 neighbor 206.206.206.1 route-map TWT-4323-INBOUND in
 neighbor 206.206.206.1 maximum-prefix 600000 95 warning-only
 no auto-summary
 no synchronization
end
```

Note the prefix-list and route-map configured within the BGP session. The prefix-list restricts what prefixes we may announce to the Internet. We can only announce /24 or larger public IP blocks that assigned by Internet address authorities and registries. In our lab, it is the 22.0.0.0/24 block. The route-map ensures what we get from our upstream providers. We want to make sure we don't get more than what we asked for because excessive amount of routing information can overwhelm the router and impact performance. maximum-prefix warning is also a good practice to let the router send out syslog warning messages when the number of prefixes received from upstream exceeded the number defined.

```
! AT&T inbound and outbound prefixes-lists
ip prefix-list ATT-7018-IN-FILTER seq 10 deny 0.0.0.0/8 le 32
ip prefix-list ATT-7018-IN-FILTER seq 20 deny 10.0.0.0/8 le 32
ip prefix-list ATT-7018-IN-FILTER seq 40 deny 127.0.0.0/8 le 32
ip prefix-list ATT-7018-IN-FILTER seq 50 deny 169.254.0.0/16 le 32
ip prefix-list ATT-7018-IN-FILTER seq 60 deny 172.16.0.0/12 le 32
ip prefix-list ATT-7018-IN-FILTER seq 70 deny 192.0.2.0/24 le 32
ip prefix-list ATT-7018-IN-FILTER seq 80 deny 192.168.0.0/16 le 32
ip prefix-list ATT-7018-IN-FILTER seq 90 deny 224.0.0.0/3 le 32
ip prefix-list ATT-7018-IN-FILTER seq 100 deny 0.0.0.0/0 ge 25
ip prefix-list ATT-7018-IN-FILTER seq 110 deny 22.0.0.0/24 le 32
ip prefix-list ATT-7018-IN-FILTER seq 9999 permit 0.0.0.0/0 le 32
!
ip prefix-list ATT-7018-OUT-FILTER seq 10 permit 22.0.0.0/24
ip prefix-list ATT-7018-OUT-FILTER seq 9999 deny 0.0.0.0/0 le 32

! TWT inbound and outbound prefixes-lists
ip prefix-list TWT-4323-IN-FILTER seq 10 deny 0.0.0.0/8 le 32
ip prefix-list TWT-4323-IN-FILTER seq 20 deny 10.0.0.0/8 le 32
ip prefix-list TWT-4323-IN-FILTER seq 40 deny 127.0.0.0/8 le 32
ip prefix-list TWT-4323-IN-FILTER seq 50 deny 169.254.0.0/16 le 32
ip prefix-list TWT-4323-IN-FILTER seq 60 deny 172.16.0.0/12 le 32
ip prefix-list TWT-4323-IN-FILTER seq 70 deny 192.0.2.0/24 le 32
ip prefix-list TWT-4323-IN-FILTER seq 80 deny 192.168.0.0/16 le 32
ip prefix-list TWT-4323-IN-FILTER seq 90 deny 224.0.0.0/3 le 32
ip prefix-list TWT-4323-IN-FILTER seq 100 deny 0.0.0.0/0 ge 25
ip prefix-list TWT-4323-IN-FILTER seq 110 deny 22.0.0.0/24 le 32
ip prefix-list TWT-4323-IN-FILTER seq 9999 permit 0.0.0.0/0 le 32
!
ip prefix-list TWT-4323-OUT-FILTER seq 10 permit 22.0.0.0/24
ip prefix-list TWT-4323-OUT-FILTER seq 9999 deny 0.0.0.0/0 le 32
```

In the inbound prefix-list, line sequence from 10 through 110 listed all the prefixes that should never appear on the Internet routing table. Those prefixes are either reserved for research purpose, multicast IP space defined by IPv4 RFC, or, private

IPs that should never be routed on the Internet. Also, if the router sees our own prefix 22.0.0.0/24 being announced by upstream provider, we do not want to inject the route ether. Once the routing information passed the prefix-list inspection, it may come in. Very often, attacks and hackers on the Internet spoof their source IPs by using one of the IPs in the list above to carry out the attacks. It is the best practice to implement an extra layer of protection when configuring BGP.

The outbound prefix-list is straightforward. It allows only our prefix 22.0.0.0/24 to be announced to the upstream Internet providers.

When you request your upstream ISP to peer with you, they will ask what types of routes you want to receive from them. Typically, there are 4 options: (or the combinations of these)

- Default route only
- Default route + ISP routes
- ISP routes + their customer routes
- Entire Internet routing table

As the time of this workbook is written, there are about 730,000 routes in the Internet routing table (ref: https://www.cidr-report.org/as2.0/#General_Status). There is no use for you to receive the entire Internet routing table unless you are an ISP providing IP transit, or for research purpose.

Although you can rely on your ISP not to send the entire Internet routing table to you, in case they messed up their configuration, we want to protect our routers. The configuration below filters the routes received from the upstream ISP and only places the ISP native routes originated from itself, and their customers' routes into our BGP routing table.

```
ip as-path access-list 1 permit ^7018_[0-9]*$
ip as-path access-list 2 permit ^4323_[0-9]*$
!
route-map ATT-7018-INBOUND permit 10
match as-path 1
route-map TWT-4323-INBOUND permit 10
match as-path 2
```

R2 has the similar configuration.

```
!R2
router bgp 65000
 bgp router-id 192.168.0.2
 bgp log-neighbor-changes
 network 22.0.0.0 mask 255.255.255.0
```

```
 redistribute static route-map STATIC->BGP
 neighbor 24.24.24.1 remote-as 20001
 neighbor 24.24.24.1 soft-reconfiguration inbound
 neighbor 24.24.24.1 prefix-list TWC-20001-IN-FILTER in
 neighbor 24.24.24.1 prefix-list TWC-20001-OUT-FILTER out
 neighbor 24.24.24.1 advertise-map ADV-MAP non-exist-map EXIST-MAP
 neighbor 24.24.24.1 maximum-prefix 600000 95 warning-only
```

For brevity, I will not spell out every configuration on R2. Check the "final.virl" file or "show run" output on a running router's CLI.

Finally, let's verify BGP neighbor relationship on R1 and R2.

```
R1#show ip bgp summary | b Neighbor
Neighbor        V          AS MsgRcvd MsgSent   TblVer  InQ OutQ Up/Down  State/PfxRcd
12.12.12.1      4        7018      51      51       18    0    0 00:39:08           1
206.206.206.1   4        4323      48      46       18    0    0 00:39:11           6
R1#
```

```
R2#show ip bgp summary | b Neighbor
Neighbor        V          AS MsgRcvd MsgSent   TblVer  InQ OutQ Up/Down  State/PfxRcd
24.24.24.1      4       20001      49      48       24    0    0 00:39:46           6
R2#
```

As you can see, R1 is peered with upstream AT&T router and TWT router, while R2 is peered with its upstream TWC router.

2. **Configure HSRP on R1 and R2's internal interface. Give R1 the preference of active Internet Gateway for internet users.**

   Shown below R1 and R2's configuration. There are two key features in this configuration:

   1. R1 is set with HSRP priority 105 (R2 uses default 100). R1 becomes the active router serving 22.0.0.1 because it has higher priority set.
   2. "track 1" is configured to watch whether the default route 0.0.0.0 /0 is still being leant from the upstream ISP. If the default route disappears, most likely it has lost upstream connection for whatever reason, all outbound traffic will stale. When that happens, a router cannot act as active gateway for users. R1 decrements 10 from its priority 105 and becomes 95. R2 has primary 100 and will take over R1's role immediately.

```
! R1
interface GigabitEthernet0/1
 description LAN
 ip address 22.0.0.2 255.255.255.0
 standby 1 ip 22.0.0.1
 standby 1 priority 105
```

```
 standby 1 preempt
 standby 1 track 1 decrement 10
end
track 1 ip route 0.0.0.0 0.0.0.0 reachability

! R2
interface GigabitEthernet0/1
 description LAN
 ip address 22.0.0.3 255.255.255.0
 standby 1 ip 22.0.0.1
 standby 1 preempt
 standby 1 track 1
end
track 1 ip route 0.0.0.0 0.0.0.0 reachability
```

Show commands verify the status of HSRP and track objects.

```
R1,R2#show standby brief
R1,R2#show track 1
```

```
R1#show standby brief
                     P indicates configured to preempt.
                     |
Interface   Grp  Pri P State    Active          Standby         Virtual IP
Gi0/1       1    105 P Active   local           22.0.0.3        22.0.0.1
R1#
R1#show track 1
Track 1
  IP route 0.0.0.0 0.0.0.0 reachability
  Reachability is Up (BGP)
    4 changes, last change 00:38:24
  First-hop interface is GigabitEthernet0/2
  Tracked by:
    HSRP GigabitEthernet0/1 1
```

```
R2#show standby brief
                     P indicates configured to preempt.
                     |
Interface   Grp  Pri P State    Active          Standby         Virtual IP
Gi0/1       1    100 P Standby  22.0.0.2        local           22.0.0.1
R2#
R2#show track 1
Track 1
  IP route 0.0.0.0 0.0.0.0 reachability
  Reachability is Up (BGP)
    2 changes, last change 00:44:27
  First-hop interface is GigabitEthernet0/2
  Tracked by:
    HSRP GigabitEthernet0/1 1
R2#
```

From the show command results we can see that R1 is the "active" router in the HSRP group while R2 is the standby router. Both routers are tracking their default gateway.

3. R2 withdraws BGP announcement unless R1 fails.

Think about the current situation for a moment. If you stopped at Step 2, all outbound traffic goes through R1 for Internet and the inbound traffic may still go through R2. Recall the requirement, we do not want any traffic to go through R2 unless R1 fails. Therefore, we need to configure conditional routing that only activates R2 when R1 fails. In other words, R2 will only perform BGP announcement when R1 fails. Otherwise, it does not announce any subnets to its BGP peers.

At this time, all the magic happens on R2. We first configure an IP SLA monitor, which keeps track of the reachability of R1's Ggi0/1 22.0.0.2. It pings R1 once every 60 seconds and repeats indefinitely. "track 2" is configured to watch "ip sla monitor 1" and declare down state after 90 seconds (track 1 is in use to track 0.0.0.0/0). Reinstate up state after 120 seconds when the monitor is up.

```
ip sla 1
 icmp-echo 22.0.0.2 source-interface GigabitEthernet0/1
ip sla schedule 1 life forever start-time now

track 2 ip sla 1 reachability
 delay down 90 up 120
```

A static Null route is used to let BGP processor know a Boolean state: true or false. The actual route does not matter. We chose to use a host route with a non-publicly routable IP. This configuration states: install the static route into our routing table only when "track 2" is up. Remove this route when "track 2" is down.

```
ip route 192.0.3.1 255.255.255.255 Null0 track 2
```

Assuming R1 is healthy, let's review R2's current status:

```
R2#show ip sla configuration 1
```

```
R2#show ip sla configuration 1
IP SLAs Infrastructure Engine-III
Entry number: 1
Owner:
Tag:
Operation timeout (milliseconds): 5000
Type of operation to perform: icmp-echo
Target address/Source interface: 22.0.0.2/GigabitEthernet0/1
Type Of Service parameter: 0x0
Request size (ARR data portion): 28
Data pattern: 0xABCDABCD
Verify data: No
Vrf Name:
Schedule:
   Operation frequency (seconds): 60  (not considered if randomly scheduled)
   Next Scheduled Start Time: Start Time already passed
   Group Scheduled : FALSE
   Randomly Scheduled : FALSE
   Life (seconds): Forever
   Entry Ageout (seconds): never
   Recurring (Starting Everyday): FALSE
   Status of entry (SNMP RowStatus): Active
Threshold (milliseconds): 5000
Distribution Statistics:
   Number of statistic hours kept: 2
   Number of statistic distribution buckets kept: 1
   Statistic distribution interval (milliseconds): 20
Enhanced History:
History Statistics:
   Number of history Lives kept: 0
   Number of history Buckets kept: 15
   History Filter Type: None
```

```
R2#show ip sla statistics
R2#show track 2
```

```
R2#show ip sla statistics
IPSLAs Latest Operation Statistics

IPSLA operation id: 1
        Latest RTT: 1 milliseconds
Latest operation start time: 23:05:00 UTC Wed Jun 6 2018
Latest operation return code: OK
Number of successes: 10
Number of failures: 0
Operation time to live: Forever
```

```
R2#show track 2
Track 2
  IP SLA 1 reachability
  Reachability is Up
    2 changes, last change 01:08:02
  Delay up 120 secs, down 90 secs
  Latest operation return code: OK
  Latest RTT (millisecs) 2
  Tracked by:
    Static IP Routing 0
R2#
```

Per our design, if the IP SLA and up and "track 2" is also Up, a static route pointing to Null shall be injected to R2. Let's see if it is true.

```
R2#show ip route static
```

```
         192.0.3.0/32 is subnetted, 1 subnets
S           192.0.3.1 is directly connected, Null0
```

Now, how does it have anything to do with BGP? In BGP configuration, we will inject the static Null route into BGP routing table with caution. Because this Null route disappears when a failure condition is met, we can use it to trigger BGP actions. Specifically, there are two conditions:

Condition 1: normal condition when R1 is up and healthy, life is good:

- "monitor 1" = OK
- "track 2" = Up
- Static Null route is present in routing table and is being redistributed into BGP table.
- BGP sees the Null route. It does NOT announce our prefix 22.0.0.0/24.

Condition 2: failure condition when R1 is down. We want to shift traffic to the backup router R2:

- "monitor 1" = Timeout
- "track 2" = DOWN
- Static Null route is withdrawn from routing table. It is no longer being redistributed into BGP table.

- BGP does NOT see the Null route. It begins announcing our prefix 22.0.0.0/24 to the world.

Here is what we need to configure on R2:

```
!R2
router bgp 65000
 no synchronization
 bgp log-neighbor-changes
 network 22.0.0.0 mask 255.255.255.0
 redistribute static route-map STATIC->BGP
 neighbor 24.24.24.1 remote-as 20001
 neighbor 24.24.24.1 soft-reconfiguration inbound
 neighbor 24.24.24.1 prefix-list TWC-20001-IN-FILTER in
 neighbor 24.24.24.1 prefix-list TWC-20001-OUT-FILTER out
 neighbor 24.24.24.1 advertise-map ADV-MAP non-exist-map EXIST-MAP
 neighbor 24.24.24.1 maximum-prefix 600000 95 warning-only
 no auto-summary
end
!
ip prefix-list PREFIX-192 seq 10 permit 192.0.3.1/32
!
route-map ADV-MAP permit 10
 match ip address prefix-list TWC-20001-OUT-FILTER
!
route-map EXIST-MAP permit 10
 match ip address prefix-list PREFIX-192
!
route-map STATIC->BGP permit 10
 match ip address prefix-list PREFIX-192
 set community no-advertise
```

To protect our BGP neighbors, we don't want the static Null route to be advertised to the BGP neighbors whatsoever. It was created as a temporary tool to interface between IP SLA and BGP conditional routing. Be careful and never redistribute any routes into BGP table unless you have a specific purpose. Even when you do, make sure the route is not leaked to elsewhere.

Now we have all the requirements configured. The next step is to verify by running through a set of testing scenarios and troubleshoot issues as they arise.

4. Validation and troubleshooting.

Here we want to validate the configuration under two scenarios. The first one is that when everything is working, we want to make sure traffic is sent and received by R1. No traffic should go through R2.

On R1, we have validated that it is the active router in HSRP cluster and is serving as the default gateway for users. R1 has two active BGP neighbors (AT&T and TWT) and it received one and six routes from each ISP respectively.

```
R1#show ip bgp summary
Neighbor          V     AS MsgRcvd MsgSent    TblVer  InQ OutQ Up/Down   PfxRcd
12.12.12.1        4   7018     109     108     18      0    0 01:31:29   1
206.206.206.1     4   4323     106     104     18      0    0 01:31:32   6
```

To see what prefixes R1 has announced to its upstream ISPs, use the commands below.

```
R1#sho ip bgp neighbors 12.12.12.1 advertised-routes
     Network           Next Hop          Metric LocPrf Weight Path
 *>  22.0.0.0/24       0.0.0.0                0         32768 i
Total number of prefixes 1

R1#sho ip bgp neighbors 206.206.206.1 advertised-routes
     Network           Next Hop          Metric LocPrf Weight Path
 *>  22.0.0.0/24       0.0.0.0                0         32768 i
```

On R2, we want to validate it has BGP neighbor relationship with the upstream provider and received prefixes. It should not advertise any route to its upstream according to the conditional routing logic we configured.

```
R2#show ip bgp summary
Neighbor          V     AS MsgRcvd MsgSent    TblVer  InQ OutQ Up/Down   PfxRcd
24.24.24.1        4  20001    113     111     24      0    0 01:37:00   6

R2#sho ip bgp neighbors 24.24.24.1 advertised-routes
Total number of prefixes 0
```

Per R2's show command output, it has received 6 prefixes from its upstream provider TWC (ASN 20001). It does not advertise any route to the upstream. By validating BGP neighbor details, the condition is not met for advertise-map, therefore status = withdraw. No route is advertised to R2's BGP neighbor.

```
R2#sho ip bgp neighbors 24.24.24.1
```

```
R2#sho ip bgp neighbors 24.24.24.1
BGP neighbor is 24.24.24.1,  remote AS 20001, external link
  BGP version 4, remote router ID 192.168.0.5
  BGP state = Established, up for 01:39:47
  Last read 00:00:33, last write 00:00:18, hold time is 180, keepalive interval is 60 seconds
  Neighbor sessions:
    1 active, is not multisession capable (disabled)
  Neighbor capabilities:
    Route refresh: advertised and received(new)
    Four-octets ASN Capability: advertised and received
    Address family IPv4 Unicast: advertised and received
    Enhanced Refresh Capability: advertised and received
    Multisession Capability:
    Stateful switchover support enabled: NO for session 1
```

```
...
For address family: IPv4 Unicast
  Session: 24.24.24.1
  BGP table version 24, neighbor version 24/0
  Output queue size : 0
  Index 1, Advertise bit 0
  1 update-group member
  Inbound soft reconfiguration allowed
  Incoming update prefix filter list is TWC-20001-IN-FILTER
  Outgoing update prefix filter list is TWC-20001-OUT-FILTER
  Condition-map EXIST-MAP, Advertise-map ADV-MAP, status: **Withdraw**
```

By now we have checked R1 and R2 and the validation results looked good. Next, let's review the routing tables on the ISP routers and see if they indeed received the 22.0.0.0/24 subnet that was announced by our R1/R2. Let's review our VIRL topology:

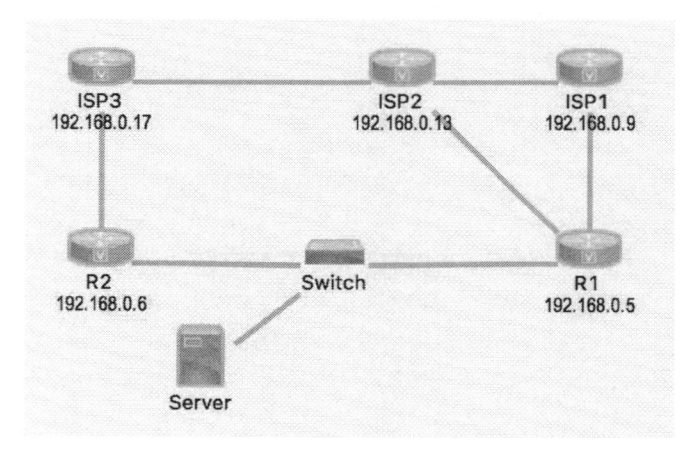

Login ISP2 and issue command "show ip bgp 22.0.0.0/24".

```
ISP2#show ip bgp 22.0.0.0/24
```

```
ISP2#show ip bgp 22.0.0.0/24
BGP routing table entry for 22.0.0.0/24, version 22
Paths: (2 available, best #2, table default)
  Advertised to update-groups:
     1
  Refresh Epoch 1
  4323 65000, (received & used)
    34.34.34.3 from 34.34.34.3 (192.168.0.3)
      Origin IGP, localpref 100, valid, external
      rx pathid: 0, tx pathid: 0
  Refresh Epoch 1
  65000, (received & used)
    12.12.12.2 from 12.12.12.2 (192.168.0.1)
      Origin IGP, metric 0, localpref 100, valid, external, best
      rx pathid: 0, tx pathid: 0x0
ISP2#
```

ISP2 did receive the routing information for 22.0.0.0/24 from both ISP1 and ISP3.

ISP3 only learned 22.0.0.0/24 from IPS2 (192.168.0.4). It is because R2 is not telling ISP3 about 22.0.0.0/24 until R1 fails. It is exactly as expected.

```
ISP3#show ip bgp 22.0.0.0/24
BGP routing table entry for 22.0.0.0/24, version 29
Paths: (1 available, best #1, table default)
  Not advertised to any peer
  Refresh Epoch 1
  7018 65000, (received & used)
    45.45.45.4 from 45.45.45.4 (192.168.0.4)
      Origin IGP, localpref 100, valid, external, best
      rx pathid: 0, tx pathid: 0x0
ISP3#
```

In order to test the overall network reachability, we created a set up dummy Internet IPs and subnets on the ISP routers. And then advertised these subnets into their BGP network via connected route redistribution. By doing so, hosts on the LAN should be able to ping these IPs.

```
ISP1#    sho ip int bri
Interface          IP-Address      OK? Method Status      Protocol
GigabitEthernet0/0 172.16.1.89     YES NVRAM  up          up
GigabitEthernet0/1 206.206.206.1   YES NVRAM  up          up
GigabitEthernet0/2 34.34.34.3      YES NVRAM  up          up
Loopback0          192.168.0.3     YES NVRAM  up          up
Loopback1          1.1.1.1         YES NVRAM  up          up
Loopback3          3.3.3.3         YES NVRAM  up          up
Loopback5          5.5.5.5         YES NVRAM  up          up
Loopback7          7.7.7.7         YES NVRAM  up          up
Loopback9          9.9.9.9         YES NVRAM  up          up
```

```
ISP2#sho ip int bri
Interface              IP-Address      OK? Method Status                Protocol
GigabitEthernet0/0     172.16.1.90     YES NVRAM  up                    up
GigabitEthernet0/1     12.12.12.1      YES NVRAM  up                    up
GigabitEthernet0/2     34.34.34.4      YES NVRAM  up                    up
GigabitEthernet0/3     45.45.45.4      YES NVRAM  up                    up
Loopback0              192.168.0.4     YES NVRAM  up                    up
Loopback2              2.2.2.2         YES NVRAM  up                    up
Loopback4              4.4.4.4         YES NVRAM  up                    up
Loopback6              6.6.6.6         YES NVRAM  up                    up
Loopback8              8.8.8.8         YES NVRAM  up                    up
Loopback10             10.10.10.10     YES NVRAM  up                    up

ISP3#sho ip int bri
Interface              IP-Address      OK? Method Status                Protocol
GigabitEthernet0/0     172.16.1.91     YES NVRAM  up                    up
GigabitEthernet0/1     24.24.24.1      YES NVRAM  up                    up
GigabitEthernet0/2     45.45.45.5      YES NVRAM  up                    up
Loopback0              192.168.0.5     YES NVRAM  up                    up
Loopback11             11.11.11.11     YES NVRAM  up                    up
Loopback33             33.33.33.33     YES NVRAM  up                    up
Loopback55             55.55.55.55     YES NVRAM  up                    up
Loopback77             77.77.77.77     YES NVRAM  up                    up
Loopback99             99.99.99.99     YES NVRAM  up                    up
```

This is how ISP1's BGP routing table looks like.

```
   Network           Next Hop          Metric LocPrf Weight Path
   0.0.0.0           0.0.0.0                             0 i
*> 1.1.1.1/32        0.0.0.0           0             32768 ?
*> 2.2.2.2/32        34.34.34.4        0                 0 7018 ?
*> 3.3.3.3/32        0.0.0.0           0             32768 ?
*> 4.4.4.4/32        34.34.34.4        0                 0 7018 ?
*> 5.5.5.5/32        0.0.0.0           0             32768 ?
*> 6.6.6.6/32        34.34.34.4        0                 0 7018 ?
*> 7.7.7.7/32        0.0.0.0           0             32768 ?
*> 8.8.8.8/32        34.34.34.4        0                 0 7018 ?
*> 9.9.9.9/32        0.0.0.0           0             32768 ?
*> 10.10.10.10/32    34.34.34.4        0                 0 7018 ?
*> 11.11.11.11/32    34.34.34.4                          0 7018 20001 ?
*> 12.12.12.0/24     34.34.34.4        0                 0 7018 ?
   Network           Next Hop          Metric LocPrf Weight Path
*  22.0.0.0/24       34.34.34.4                          0 7018 65000 i
*>                   206.206.206.2     0                 0 65000 i
*> 24.24.24.0/24     34.34.34.4                          0 7018 20001 ?
*> 33.33.33.33/32    34.34.34.4                          0 7018 20001 ?
*  34.34.34.0/24     34.34.34.4        0                 0 7018 ?
*>                   0.0.0.0           0             32768 ?
*> 45.45.45.0/24     34.34.34.4        0                 0 7018 ?
*> 55.55.55.55/32    34.34.34.4                          0 7018 20001 ?
*> 77.77.77.77/32    34.34.34.4                          0 7018 20001 ?
*> 99.99.99.99/32    34.34.34.4                          0 7018 20001 ?
*  172.16.1.0/24     34.34.34.4        0                 0 7018 ?
*>                   0.0.0.0           0             32768 ?
*> 192.168.0.3/32    0.0.0.0           0             32768 ?
*> 192.168.0.4/32    34.34.34.4        0                 0 7018 ?
*> 192.168.0.5/32    34.34.34.4                          0 7018 20001 ?
*> 206.206.206.0     0.0.0.0           0             32768 ?
```

On the Linux server, we can test by pinging these Internet IP addresses generated by the ISP routers.

```
cisco@Server:~$ ping 1.1.1.1
PING 1.1.1.1 (1.1.1.1) 56(84) bytes of data.
64 bytes from 1.1.1.1: icmp_seq=2 ttl=254 time=5.78 ms
64 bytes from 1.1.1.1: icmp_seq=3 ttl=254 time=7.61 ms
From 172.16.1.94 icmp_seq=1 Destination Host Unreachable
64 bytes from 1.1.1.1: icmp_seq=4 ttl=254 time=4.93 ms
^C
--- 1.1.1.1 ping statistics ---
4 packets transmitted, 3 received, +1 errors, 25% packet loss, time 3004ms
rtt min/avg/max/mdev = 4.930/6.108/7.611/1.118 ms, pipe 4
cisco@Server:~$ ping 2.2.2.2
PING 2.2.2.2 (2.2.2.2) 56(84) bytes of data.
64 bytes from 2.2.2.2: icmp_seq=1 ttl=254 time=9.99 ms
64 bytes from 2.2.2.2: icmp_seq=2 ttl=254 time=4.52 ms
64 bytes from 2.2.2.2: icmp_seq=3 ttl=254 time=4.92 ms
^C
--- 2.2.2.2 ping statistics ---
3 packets transmitted, 3 received, 0% packet loss, time 2003ms
rtt min/avg/max/mdev = 4.524/6.482/9.994/2.488 ms
```

On the Linux server, let's do a "traceroute" (on the Ubuntu server, use "tracepath" instead) to IP address 11.11.11.11. This IP is advertised by ISP3. The packet is going through R1, ISP1, ISP2 to reach ISP3. It is working as expected.

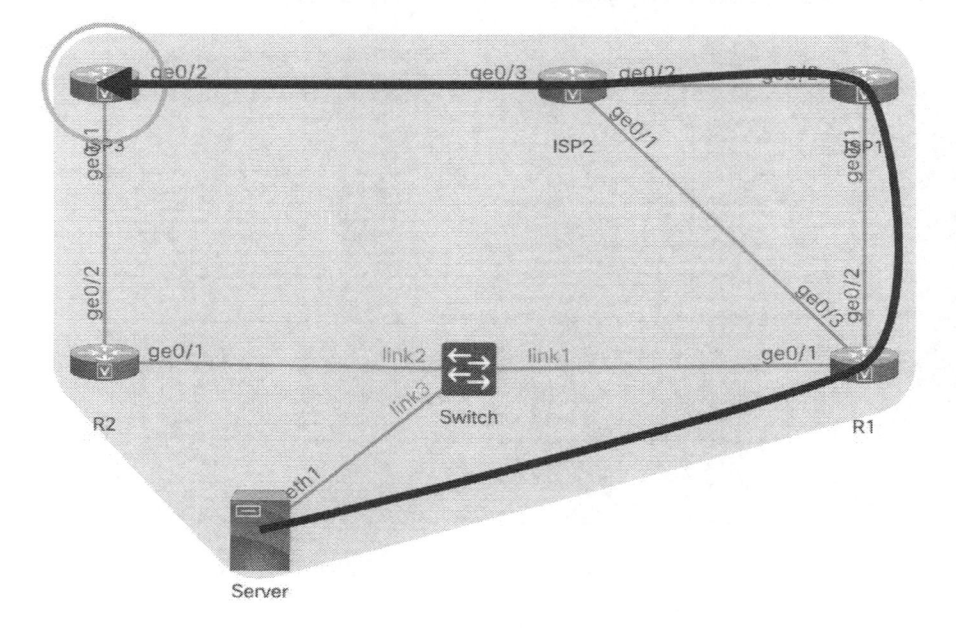

```
cisco@Server:~$ tracepath 11.11.11.11          ISP3
 1?: [LOCALHOST]                                        pmtu 1500
 1:  22.0.0.2        R1                                 2.344ms
 1:  22.0.0.2                                           2.281ms
 2:  206.206.206.1   ISP1                               4.949ms
 3:  34.34.34.4      ISP2                               8.199ms asymm  2
 4:  45.45.45.5      ISP3                               9.117ms reached
     Resume: pmtu 1500 hops 4 back 3
```

The second scenario we wanted validate is that when R1 fails, R2 should take over and make announcement to the world that he is now in charge. In order to test, we introduced a failure condition by shutting down R1. In VM Maestro, right-click on R1 and select "Stop this node". Make sure you extract the configuration before stopping the node so that its configuration will not be lost.

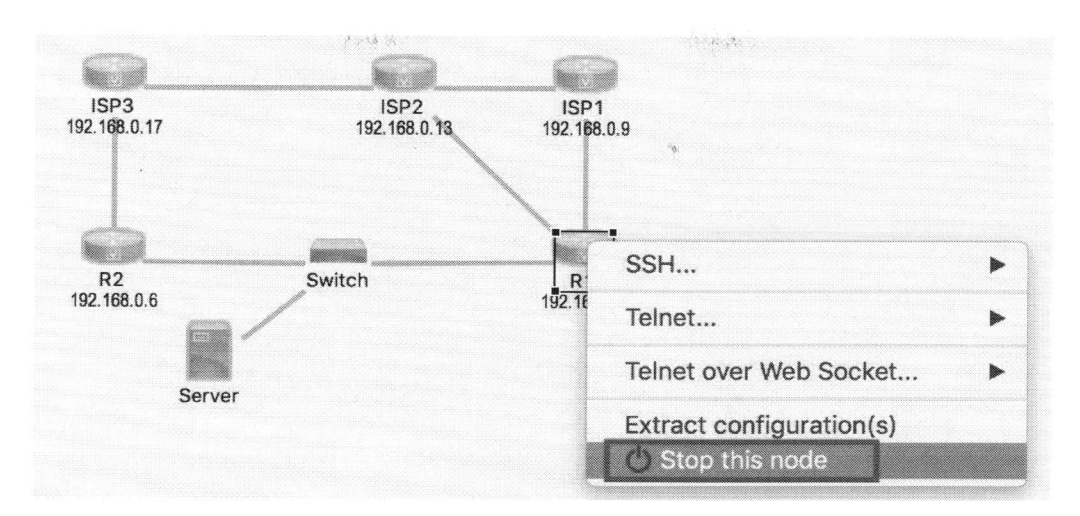

Looking into R2's neighbor details, we found that the advertise-map condition has been met and our prefix is now advertised to R2's upstream.

```
R2#
*Jun  6 23:56:44.149: %GRUB-5-CONFIG_WRITING: GRUB configuration is being updated on disk. Please wait...
*Jun  6 23:56:45.090: %GRUB-5-CONFIG_WRITTEN: GRUB configuration was written to disk successfully.
*Jun  6 23:57:37.305: %HSRP-5-STATECHANGE: GigabitEthernet0/1 Grp 1 state Standby -> Active
```

```
R2#
R2#show standby brief
                     P indicates configured to preempt.
                     |
Interface   Grp  Pri P State    Active          Standby         Virtual IP
Gi0/1       1    100 P Active   local           unknown         22.0.0.1
```

```
R2#sho ip bgp neighbors 24.24.24.1
BGP neighbor is 24.124.24.1, remote AS 20001, external link
...
For address family: IPv4 Unicast
BGP table version 45956558, neighbor version 45956542/0
Output queue size : 0
Index 1, Offset 0, Mask 0x2
1 update-group member
Inbound soft reconfiguration allowed
Incoming update prefix filter list is TWC-20001-IN-FILTER
Outgoing update prefix filter list is TWC-20001-OUT-FILTER
Condition-map EXIST-MAP, Advertise-map ADV-MAP, status: **Advertise**
```

Now R2 is announcing the 22.0.0.0/24 prefix to the Internet (ISP3) on R1's behalf.

```
R2#sho ip bgp neighbors 24.24.24.1 advertised-routes
BGP table version is 49, local router ID is 192.168.0.2
Status codes: s suppressed, d damped, h history, * valid, > best, i - internal,
              r RIB-failure, S Stale, m multipath, b backup-path, f RT-Filter,
              x best-external, a additional-path, c RIB-compressed,
              t secondary path,
Origin codes: i - IGP, e - EGP, ? - incomplete
RPKI validation codes: V valid, I invalid, N Not found

     Network          Next Hop            Metric LocPrf Weight Path
 *>  22.0.0.0/24      0.0.0.0                  0         32768 i

Total number of prefixes 1
```

Let's make sure the Linux server still can ping the Internet IPs.

```
cisco@Server:~$ ping 11.11.11.11
PING 11.11.11.11 (11.11.11.11) 56(84) bytes of data.
64 bytes from 11.11.11.11: icmp_seq=1 ttl=254 time=2.86 ms
64 bytes from 11.11.11.11: icmp_seq=2 ttl=254 time=3.53 ms
64 bytes from 11.11.11.11: icmp_seq=3 ttl=254 time=3.91 ms
^C
--- 11.11.11.11 ping statistics ---
3 packets transmitted, 3 received, 0% packet loss, time 2003ms
rtt min/avg/max/mdev = 2.869/3.440/3.915/0.437 ms
cisco@Server:~$ ping 99.99.99.99
PING 99.99.99.99 (99.99.99.99) 56(84) bytes of data.
64 bytes from 99.99.99.99: icmp_seq=1 ttl=254 time=3.80 ms
64 bytes from 99.99.99.99: icmp_seq=2 ttl=254 time=2.68 ms
64 bytes from 99.99.99.99: icmp_seq=3 ttl=254 time=3.10 ms
^C
--- 99.99.99.99 ping statistics ---
3 packets transmitted, 3 received, 0% packet loss, time 2003ms
rtt min/avg/max/mdev = 2.686/3.196/3.801/0.460 ms
```

Ping looked good. Finally, we want to see the outbound traffic is going through R2. We can validate it by using traceroute from the Linux server to 11.11.11.11 on ISP3.

```
cisco@Server:~$ tracepath 11.11.11.11   ISP3
 1?: [LOCALHOST]                                        pmtu 1500
 1:  22.0.0.3   R2                                      4.310ms
 1:  22.0.0.3                                           5.344ms
 2:  24.24.24.1  ISP3                                   3.119ms reached
     Resume: pmtu 1500 hops 2 back 2
```

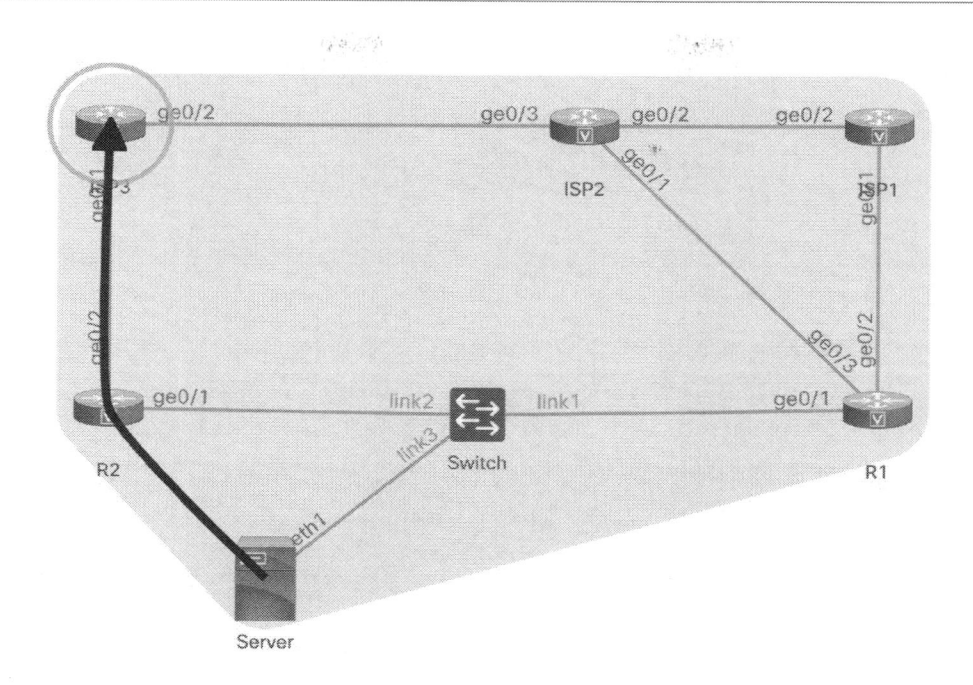

It worked exactly as designed. Congratulations and you have completed this lab.

Topology 8: Configuring DMVPN With IPSec and EIGRP Overlay

Overview

The Dynamic Multipoint VPN (DMVPN) is one of the best solutions to the increasing demands of enterprise companies to be able to connect branch offices with headquarters and between each other while keeping costs low, minimizing configuration complexity and increasing flexibility. DMVPN allows users to scale by combining generic routing encapsulation (GRE) tunnels, IPSec encryption, and Next Hop Resolution Protocol (NHRP) to provide users with easy configuration through crypto profiles, which eliminate the requirement for defining static crypto maps, and dynamic discovery of tunnel endpoints.

Here are the main benefits of deploying DMVPN.

- Simplified Hub Router Configuration. No more multiple tunnel interfaces for each branch (spoke) VPN. A single mGRE, IPSec profile without any crypto access lists, is all that is required to handle all Spoke routers. No matter how many Spoke routers connect to the Hub, the Hub configuration remains the same.
- Support for Spoke Routers with Dynamic Public IP Addresses. A perfect solution for small branch offices and home offices without static public IPs.
- Dynamic Creation of Spoke-to-Spoke VPN Tunnels. Spoke routers are able to dynamically create VPN Tunnels among them without sending traffic to the hub. The tunnels are created on-demand.
- Strong Security with IPSec. Optionally, IPSec can be configured to provide data encryption and confidentiality. IPSec is used to secure the mGRE tunnels by encrypting the tunnel traffic using encryption algorithms.
- Lower Costs. Remember last time you had to configure new VPN tunnels every time there is a branch office opens? Or when the ISP changed public IP on you, you had to update the hub configuration each time? DMVPN simplifies the hub configuration. You don't need to change the configuration each time when there is a new spoke comes online. Furthermore, the spoke router's configuration is mostly the same. You can build a template and stand up a remote site with no time.

Network Topology

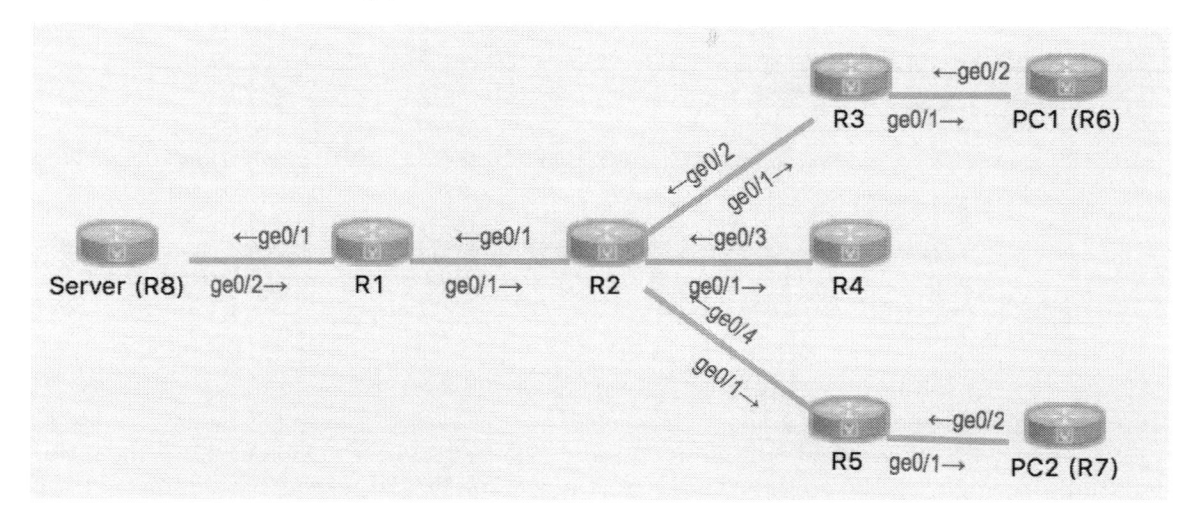

The network topology includes eight routers. R1 is the hub router at the headquarters. R3, R4 and R5 are the spoke routers at branch offices. R2 is an Internet transit router. We mimic branch office PCs using R6 and R7, and a Server using R8 at HQ. They are used perform Ping and Traceroute testing.

What has been done in the initial configuration:

- Wiring among the routers
- Host names
- OOB management and Loopback0 IP addresses
- Underlay OSPF routing among WAN routers: R1, R2, R3, R4 and R5
- Static default gateway has been configured on R6, R7 and R8 pointing to their upstream routers.
- Username / Password for routers: cisco / cisco

Requirements

1. Configure a DMVPN network among R1, R3, R4, and R5. R1 should be the hub and R3, R4, and R5 the spokes. Use router's physical interface as the tunnel source.
2. Use the IP addresses 10.1.1.X/24 inside the tunnel, where X is the router number.
3. Configure R1 to advertise just a default route to the DMVPN spokes via EIGRP.
4. Enable NHRP authentication and use key "VIRLBOOK". Activate DMVPN Phase 3 support.

5. When DMVPN is established, ensure that participating routers can reach each other over the DMVPN network.
6. R6 and R7 should have reachability to each other. The traffic should *not* go through the hub R1.
7. For enhanced security, configure IPsec over the DMVPN network using the following parameters.
    - ISAKMP Policy: Pre-Shared Key: "VIRLBOOKPSK", Encryption: AES 256 Bit, Hash: SHA 256 Bit, Diffie-Hellman Group: 2
    - IPsec Profile: IPsec Encapsulation: ESP Transport Mode, Encryption: AES 256 Bit, Hash: SHA 512 Bit
8. To avoid IPsec fragmentation, configure the GRE tunnel's IP MTU to 1400 bytes, and set them to adjust the TCP MSS accordingly.
9. As a result, hub-to-spoke and spoke-to-spoke IPsec tunnels should form on-demand. Ensure traffic between spokes should not be forwarded to the hub.

Solutions

There are four major steps to configure DMVPN:

1. Configure the Hub router
2. Configure the Spoke router(s)
3. Configure routing inside the VPN tunnels using dynamic or static routing protocol
4. Encrypt VPN traffic with IPSec (optional)

The Hub router is configured as a NHRP "server", where all the Spoke routers register to it as NHRP clients. A GRE tunnel is then built between the Spoke and Hub routers. A Spoke router may also form a VPN tunnel with another Spoke router. All routers run multipoint GRE (mGRE) since the tunnels are point-to-multipoint in nature. When a Spoke router needs to send a packet to a destination subnet on another Spoke, it queries the NHRP server (the Hub) for the IP address of the destination Spoke router. After the sending Spoke learns the peer address of the destination Spoke, it can initiate a dynamic tunnel to the destination Spoke. The spoke-to-spoke tunnel is built over the multipoint GRE (mGRE) interface. The spoke-to-spoke tunnels are established on demand whenever there is traffic between the Spokes. Thereafter, packets sent and received directly between Spokes without having to go through the Hub. Finally, if you want to encrypt traffic for confidentiality, configure IPSec on top of the DMVPN tunnels.

The key technologies that enabled DMVPN are mGRE and NHRP. Traditional GRE tunnel is point-to-point, while mGRE generalizes this idea by allowing a tunnel to have "multiple" destinations. NHRP is used to map tunnel IP addresses to "physical" or "real"

IP addresses. NHRP is similar in function to ARP, allowing resolving L3 to L2 addresses, but does that in partially meshed NBMA cloud supporting dynamic layer 2 connections.

1. Configure DMVPN Hub router R1 and make it a NHRP server.

On R1, configure Tunnel0 as a logical interface to terminate all mGRE tunnels. The tunnel interface itself shall have an IP address as well.

```
!R1
interface Tunnel0
 description DMVPN Hub
 ip address 10.1.1.1 255.255.255.0
 no ip redirects
 ip nhrp authentication VIRLBOOK
 ip nhrp map multicast dynamic
 ip nhrp network-id 1
 tunnel source GigabitEthernet0/1
 tunnel mode gre multipoint
 tunnel key 2
end
```

Notice that the configuration is very similar to a traditional GRE tunnel expect there is no "tunnel destination" specified. It is because the destination is replaced by "tunnel mode gre multipoint", preparing itself to accept multiple GRE destinations.

"ip nhrp map multicast dynamic" defines R1 as a Next-Hop Server. The NHRP server is used to create mappings between the public IP address used for the tunnel source and the private IP address used inside of the tunnel, which is simply called the tunnel address.

"ip nhrp network-id 1" defines a particular NHRP network. All routers participating in a DMVPN network should have the same ID number.

"ip nhrp authentication" adds a layer of security, it is used to allow the authenticated updates and queries to the NHRP Database, ensuring unwanted queries are not provided with any information about the DMVPN network.

2. Configure DMVPN Spoke routers, R3, R4 and R5.

On R3, the mGRE tunnel has very similar configuration to the Hub router. The best practice is to use its Internet facing physical interface as source of the tunnel. It provides greater flexibility for the spokes with dynamic WAN IP addresses. When the Spoke's WAN IP changes, it will be able to update the Next-Hop server with its new WAN IP address. The Spoke routers use NHRP to inform the hub about dynamically appearing spokes.

```
!R3
interface Tunnel0
 description DMVPN Spoke
 ip address 10.1.1.3 255.255.255.0
 no ip redirects
 ip nhrp authentication VIRLBOOK
 ip nhrp map 10.1.1.1 22.1.12.1
 ip nhrp map multicast 22.1.12.1
 ip nhrp network-id 1
 ip nhrp nhs 10.1.1.1
 tunnel source GigabitEthernet0/1
 tunnel mode gre multipoint
 tunnel key 2
end
```

"ip nhrp nhs 10.1.1.1" specifies the Next-Hop Server IP that the Spoke uses to reach.

"ip nhrp map multicast 22.1.12.1" specifies the destination that will receive the multicast traffic originated from this router. Spokes map multicasts to the static IP address of the hub. The hub then replicates multicast packets to all spokes registered with NHRP. Mapping multicasts is important in order to make dynamic routing protocol establish adjacencies and exchange update packets.

On other Spoke routers, the only configuration difference is the Tunnel0's IP address itself. Now you see the benefit of deploying DMVPN, where the configuration of a branch routers is mostly the same.

```
!R4
interface Tunnel0
 description DMVPN Spoke
 ip address 10.1.1.4 255.255.255.0
 no ip redirects
 ip nhrp authentication VIRLBOOK
 ip nhrp map 10.1.1.1 22.1.12.1
 ip nhrp map multicast 22.1.12.1
 ip nhrp network-id 1
 ip nhrp nhs 10.1.1.1
 tunnel source GigabitEthernet0/1
 tunnel mode gre multipoint
 tunnel key 2
end

!R5
interface Tunnel0
 description DMVPN Spoke
 ip address 10.1.1.5 255.255.255.0
 no ip redirects
```

```
    ip nhrp authentication VIRLBOOK
    ip nhrp map 10.1.1.1 22.1.12.1
    ip nhrp map multicast 22.1.12.1
    ip nhrp network-id 1
    ip nhrp nhs 10.1.1.1
    tunnel source GigabitEthernet0/1
    tunnel mode gre multipoint
    tunnel key 2
end
```

```
*Jun 24 21:40:28.083: %SYS-5-CONFIG_I: Configured from console by console
*Jun 24 21:40:28.549: %LINEPROTO-5-UPDOWN: Line protocol on Interface Tunnel0, changed state to up
R5#
```

```
R5#sho ip int bri
Interface              IP-Address      OK? Method Status    Protocol
GigabitEthernet0/0     172.16.1.138    YES NVRAM  up        up
GigabitEthernet0/1     22.1.25.5       YES manual up        up
GigabitEthernet0/2     22.1.57.5       YES manual up        up
Loopback0              5.5.5.5         YES manual up        up
Tunnel0                10.1.1.5        YES manual up        up
```

3. Verify DMVPN functionality

Verify DMVPN status on the Hub router R1. The output of the show command displays the NHRP peer's Internet facing IP address and Tunnel IP address. On R1, we can see it has formed peers with R3, R4 and R5.

```
R1#show dmvpn
```

```
R1#show dmvpn
Legend: Attrb --> S - Static, D - Dynamic, I - Incomplete
        N - NATed, L - Local, X - No Socket
        T1 - Route Installed, T2 - Nexthop-override
        C - CTS Capable
        # Ent --> Number of NHRP entries with same NBMA peer
        NHS Status: E --> Expecting Replies, R --> Responding, W --> Waiting
        UpDn Time --> Up or Down Time for a Tunnel
==========================================================================

Interface: Tunnel0, IPv4 NHRP Details
Type:Hub, NHRP Peers:3,

 # Ent  Peer NBMA Addr Peer Tunnel Add State  UpDn Tm Attrb
 ----- --------------- --------------- ----- -------- -----
     1 22.1.23.3             10.1.1.3    UP 00:34:23     D
     1 22.1.24.4             10.1.1.4    UP 00:15:18     D
     1 22.1.25.5             10.1.1.5    UP 00:15:06     D
```

Notice the tunnel State is UP and how long it has been up for. "D" attribute indicates that this tunnel was Dynamically established.

On the Spoke routers, we can find similar results except the tunnel attribute shows "S". It is because we configured NHS IP on the Spoke routers. The configuration makes the Spoke router to go and find the Hub router on the Internet. In other words, the Hub never goes out to look for Spokes.

```
R3#show dmvpn
Legend: Attrb --> S - Static, D - Dynamic, I - Incomplete
        N - NATed, L - Local, X - No Socket
        T1 - Route Installed, T2 - Nexthop-override
        C - CTS Capable
        # Ent --> Number of NHRP entries with same NBMA peer
        NHS Status: E --> Expecting Replies, R --> Responding, W --> Waiting
        UpDn Time --> Up or Down Time for a Tunnel
==========================================================================

Interface: Tunnel0, IPv4 NHRP Details
Type:Spoke, NHRP Peers:1,

 # Ent  Peer NBMA Addr Peer Tunnel Add State  UpDn Tm Attrb
 ----- --------------- --------------- ----- -------- -----
     1 22.1.12.1             10.1.1.1   UP 00:36:46     S
```

4. Enable DMVPN Phase 3, EIGRP and adjust MTU

The basic DMVPN tunnels are up. We need to configure the Hub to redirect NHRP requests for spoke-to-spoke resolutions. DMVPN phase 3 increases scalability of the network by minimizing the amount of routing information and updates that the spokes need to maintain, while still allowing for on-demand spoke-to-spoke tunnels. We'll enable EIGRP routing inside the DMVPN tunnels while only letting the Hub router send a default route over the tunnel to the spoke via EIGRP.

On the Hub router R1 under Tunnel 0 interface configuration, enable NHRP redirect. The NHRP redirect message is an indication that the current path to the destination is not optimal. The receiver of the message should find a better path to the destination – build a spoke-to-spoke tunnel and go directly.

```
!R1
interface Tunnel0
 ip nhrp redirect
 ...
```

Activate EIGRP routing inside the DMVPN tunnel. The Hub router R1 shall only announce a default route to the Spokes. Here we use named EIGRP configuration and configure address-family for IPv4.

All interfaces are set as "passive-interface". Only "Tunnel0" interface is allowed to participate and form EIGRP neighbor relationship. Since R1 is a Hub, it announces a default route 0.0.0.0 0.0.0.0 in the EIGRP routing table. R3, R4 and R5 will receive this default route and send all traffic to R1 for outbound.

```
!R1
router eigrp MYDMVPN
 !
 address-family ipv4 unicast autonomous-system 1
  !
  af-interface default
   passive-interface
  exit-af-interface
  !
  af-interface Tunnel0
   summary-address 0.0.0.0 0.0.0.0
   no passive-interface
  exit-af-interface
  !
  topology base
  exit-af-topology
  network 10.1.1.0 0.0.0.255
 exit-address-family
```

On R3, R4 and R5, Tunnel0 interfaces will need to be made non-passive to participate in EIGRP routing. Unlike the Hub router that needed to inject a default route, the Spoke routers need to notify what local subnets they have to the central office (Hub). For example, on R3, "network 22.1.36.0 0.0.0.255" announces its local subnet 22.1.36.0/24 into EIGRP routing table. R5 would do the same. R4 does not have a local subnet for this lab setup.

```
!R3
router eigrp MYDMVPN
 !
 address-family ipv4 unicast autonomous-system 1
  !
  af-interface default
   passive-interface
  exit-af-interface
  !
  af-interface Tunnel0
   no passive-interface
```

```
  exit-af-interface
  !
  topology base
  exit-af-topology
  network 10.1.1.0 0.0.0.255
  network 22.1.36.0 0.0.0.255
 exit-address-family

!R4
router eigrp MYDMVPN
 !
 address-family ipv4 unicast autonomous-system 1
  !
  af-interface default
   passive-interface
  exit-af-interface
  !
  af-interface Tunnel0
   no passive-interface
  exit-af-interface
  !
  topology base
  exit-af-topology
  network 10.1.1.0 0.0.0.255
 exit-address-family

!R5
router eigrp MYDMVPN
 !
 address-family ipv4 unicast autonomous-system 1
  !
  af-interface default
   passive-interface
  exit-af-interface
  !
  af-interface Tunnel0
   no passive-interface
  exit-af-interface
  !
  topology base
  exit-af-topology
  network 10.1.1.0 0.0.0.255
  network 22.1.57.0 0.0.0.255
 exit-address-family
```

EIGRP neighbors are coming up over Tunnel0 interfaces.

```
R1#
*Jun 30 12:54:29.285: %DUAL-5-NBRCHANGE: EIGRP-IPv4 1: Neighbor 10.1.1.3 (Tunnel0) is up: new adjacency
*Jun 30 12:54:33.361: %DUAL-5-NBRCHANGE: EIGRP-IPv4 1: Neighbor 10.1.1.4 (Tunnel0) is up: new adjacency
*Jun 30 12:54:36.602: %DUAL-5-NBRCHANGE: EIGRP-IPv4 1: Neighbor 10.1.1.5 (Tunnel0) is up: new adjacency
```

Verify EIGRP neighbor relationship on R1 and exam its routing table. Make sure R3 and R5's local subnets can be seen.

```
R1#show ip eigrp neighbors
R1#show ip route eigrp
```

```
R1#sho ip eigrp neighbors
EIGRP-IPv4 VR(MYDMVPN) Address-Family Neighbors for AS(1)
H   Address                 Interface       Hold Uptime   SRTT   RTO  Q   Seq
                                            (sec)         (ms)        Cnt Num
1   10.1.1.5                Tu0              11 00:43:31   22   1470  0   13
0   10.1.1.4                Tu0              13 00:43:40  994   5000  0   11
2   10.1.1.3                Tu0              10 00:43:50   12   1470  0   13
```

```
R1#sho ip route eigrp
Codes: L - local, C - connected, S - static, R - RIP, M - mobile, B - BGP
       D - EIGRP, EX - EIGRP external, O - OSPF, IA - OSPF inter area
       N1 - OSPF NSSA external type 1, N2 - OSPF NSSA external type 2
       E1 - OSPF external type 1, E2 - OSPF external type 2
       i - IS-IS, su - IS-IS summary, L1 - IS-IS level-1, L2 - IS-IS level-2
       ia - IS-IS inter area, * - candidate default, U - per-user static route
       o - ODR, P - periodic downloaded static route, H - NHRP, l - LISP
       a - application route
       + - replicated route, % - next hop override, p - overrides from PfR

Gateway of last resort is 0.0.0.0 to network 0.0.0.0

D*      0.0.0.0/0 is a summary, 00:38:40, Null0
        22.0.0.0/8 is variably subnetted, 9 subnets, 2 masks
D          22.1.36.0/24 [90/76805120] via 10.1.1.3, 00:32:02, Tunnel0
D          22.1.57.0/24 [90/76805120] via 10.1.1.5, 00:29:58, Tunnel0
```

To prevent the tunnel endpoints from having to do IPsec fragmentation, configure the GRE tunnel's IP MTU to 1400 bytes, and set them to adjust the TCP MSS accordingly.

```
!R1, R3, R4, R5
interface Tunnel0
 ip mtu 1400
 ip tcp adjust-mss 1360
```

Configuration of DMVPN phase 3 with EIGRP has been completed. In the next step, we'll verify the tunnels are built correctly, and spoke-to-spoke tunnels will be constructed on-demand.

5. DMVPN tunnel verifications

Here we will use our PC1 (R6), PC2 (R7) and Server (R8) to test the DMVPN connectivity. First let's make sure the Hub router R1 at HQ office can see all remote branch offices.

This command verifies R1 has tunnels to every branch office and the status is Up.

```
R1#show dmvp
```

```
R1#show dmvp
Legend: Attrb --> S - Static, D - Dynamic, I - Incomplete
        N - NATed, L - Local, X - No Socket
        T1 - Route Installed, T2 - Nexthop-override
        C - CTS Capable
        # Ent --> Number of NHRP entries with same NBMA peer
        NHS Status: E --> Expecting Replies, R --> Responding, W --> Waiting
        UpDn Time --> Up or Down Time for a Tunnel
==========================================================================

Interface: Tunnel0, IPv4 NHRP Details
Type:Hub, NHRP Peers:3,

 # Ent  Peer NBMA Addr Peer Tunnel Add State  UpDn Tm Attrb
 ----- --------------- --------------- ----- -------- -----
     1 22.1.23.3              10.1.1.3    UP    5d15h     D
     1 22.1.24.4              10.1.1.4    UP    5d15h     D
     1 22.1.25.5              10.1.1.5    UP    5d15h     D
```

Login R8, with which we use to mimic a server at the HQ and verify the network connectivity to the remote office PCs. We can ping PC1 and PC2 across the DMVPN tunnels.

```
Server-R8#ping 22.1.36.6
Type escape sequence PC1 (R6) abort.
Sending 5, 100-byte ICMP Echos to 22.1.36.6, timeout is 2 seconds:
!!!!!
Success rate is 100 percent (5/5), round-trip min/avg/max = 5/9/16 ms
Server-R8#
Server-R8#ping 22.1.57.7
Type escape sequence PC2 (R7) abort.
Sending 5, 100-byte ICMP Echos to 22.1.57.7, timeout is 2 seconds:
!!!!!
Success rate is 100 percent (5/5), round-trip min/avg/max = 7/11/14 ms
```

Login R3 and confirm the only tunnel is has is with the Hub router R1.

```
R3#show dmvpn
```

```
# Ent  Peer NBMA Addr  Peer Tunnel Add  State  UpDn Tm  Attrb
-----  --------------  ---------------  -----  -------  -----
    1  22.1.12.1 R1         10.1.1.1    UP     5d15h      S
R3#
```

Logon R3 and ping R5. The ping traffic initiated on R3 is supposed to trigger it to talk to the Hub about how to get to R5. R1 uses NHRP to look up its mapping database and found R5 is one of its connected Spokes. R1 then tells R3 how to get to R5 directly. R3 receives the intelligence and checks in with R5. R5 welcomes R3 and a dynamic tunnel is now setup between R3 and R5.

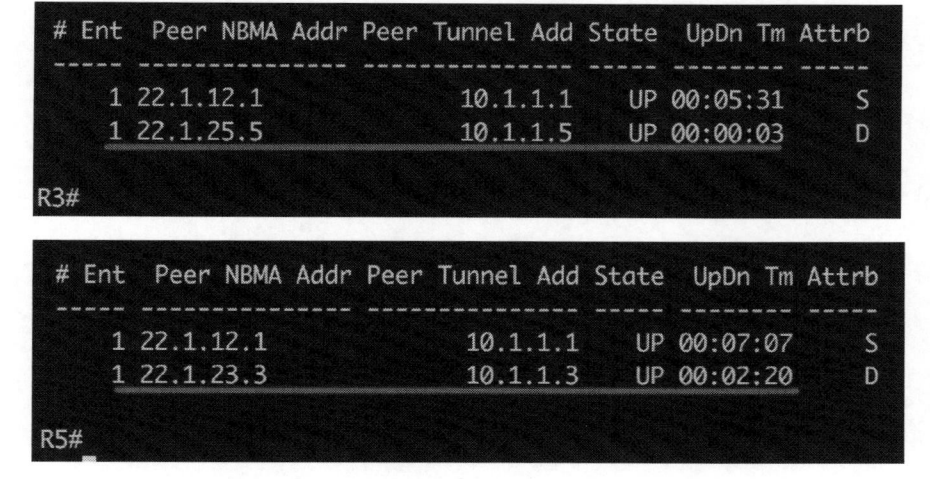

```
# Ent  Peer NBMA Addr  Peer Tunnel Add  State  UpDn Tm   Attrb
-----  --------------  ---------------  -----  --------  -----
    1  22.1.12.1            10.1.1.1    UP     00:05:31    S
    1  22.1.25.5            10.1.1.5    UP     00:00:03    D
R3#
```

```
# Ent  Peer NBMA Addr  Peer Tunnel Add  State  UpDn Tm   Attrb
-----  --------------  ---------------  -----  --------  -----
    1  22.1.12.1            10.1.1.1    UP     00:07:07    S
    1  22.1.23.3            10.1.1.3    UP     00:02:20    D
R5#
```

Logon to PC1 (R6) and now you can ping PC2 (R7).

```
PC1-R6#ping 22.1.57.7
```

```
PC1-R6#ping 22.1.57.7
Type escape sequence to abort.
Sending 5, 100-byte ICMP Echos to 22.1.57.7, timeout is 2 seconds:
!!!!!
Success rate is 100 percent (5/5), round-trip min/avg/max = 10/12/17 ms
PC1-R6#
```

We have verified the DMVPN is working. The final step is to encrypt the tunnel traffic with IPSec.

6. Encrypt tunnel traffic with IPSec.

IPSec can be used in conjunction with GRE to provide security encryption for our data, thereby providing a complete secure and flexible VPN solution. With GRE IPSec transport mode, the GRE packet is encapsulated and encrypted inside the IPSec packet and the GRE IP Header is placed at the front. If you have configured

ASA for IPSec VPN, the configuration will be very similar. Let's first configure the Hub router R1.

```
!R1
crypto isakmp policy 5
 encr aes 256
 hash sha256
 authentication pre-share
 group 2
crypto isakmp key VIRLBOOKPSK address 0.0.0.0
!
!
crypto ipsec transform-set ESP-AES-256-SHA-512 esp-aes 256 esp-sha512-hmac
 mode transport
!
crypto ipsec profile MY_DMVPN
 set transform-set ESP-AES-256-SHA-512
!
interface Tunnel 0
 tunnel protection ipsec profile MY_DMVPN
exit
```

"crypto isakmp key VIRLBOOKPSK address **0.0.0.0**" defines an ISAKMP key and valid peer IP address. Since the branch offices can have dynamic public IP addresses, and new offices can be set up in the future, we use 0.0.0.0. It accepts any peer has the right key. The Spoke routers will use 0.0.0.0 as well although the Hub has a static IP. It is because spoke-to-spoke tunnels can be built on-demand and their IP addresses may change.

IPSec profile MY_DMVPN is defined in global configuration and referenced under Tunnel 0 interface configuration. The Spoke routers

```
!R3, R4, R5
crypto isakmp policy 5
 encr aes 256
 hash sha256
 authentication pre-share
 group 2
crypto isakmp key VIRLBOOKPSK address 0.0.0.0
!
!
crypto ipsec transform-set ESP-AES-256-SHA-512 esp-aes 256 esp-sha512-hmac
 mode transport
!
```

```
crypto ipsec profile MY_DMVPN
 set transform-set ESP-AES-256-SHA-512
!
interface Tunnel 0
 tunnel protection ipsec profile MY_DMVPN
exit
```

Finally verify the IPSec crypto sessions are up and protecting traffic.

On R1 check crypto isakmp SA are up with Spoke routers.

```
R1#show crypto isakmp sa
```

```
R1#      show crypto isakmp sa
IPv4 Crypto ISAKMP SA
dst             src             state           conn-id status
22.1.25.5       22.1.12.1       QM_IDLE            1002 ACTIVE
22.1.12.1       22.1.24.4       QM_IDLE            1004 ACTIVE
22.1.12.1       22.1.23.3       QM_IDLE            1003 ACTIVE
22.1.12.1       22.1.25.5       QM_IDLE            1001 ACTIVE
22.1.23.3       22.1.12.1       QM_IDLE            1005 ACTIVE
22.1.24.4       22.1.12.1       QM_IDLE            1006 ACTIVE

IPv6 Crypto ISAKMP SA
```

```
R1#show crypto session
```

```
R1#show crypto session
Crypto session current status

Interface: Tunnel0
Session status: UP-ACTIVE
Peer: 22.1.25.5 port 500
  Session ID: 0
  IKEv1 SA: local 22.1.12.1/500 remote 22.1.25.5/500 Active
  Session ID: 0
  IKEv1 SA: local 22.1.12.1/500 remote 22.1.25.5/500 Active
  IPSEC FLOW: permit 47 host 22.1.12.1 host 22.1.25.5
        Active SAs: 4, origin: crypto map

Interface: Tunnel0
Session status: UP-ACTIVE
Peer: 22.1.24.4 port 500
  Session ID: 0
  IKEv1 SA: local 22.1.12.1/500 remote 22.1.24.4/500 Active
  Session ID: 0
  IKEv1 SA: local 22.1.12.1/500 remote 22.1.24.4/500 Active
  IPSEC FLOW: permit 47 host 22.1.12.1 host 22.1.24.4
        Active SAs: 4, origin: crypto map

Interface: Tunnel0
Session status: UP-ACTIVE
Peer: 22.1.23.3 port 500
  Session ID: 0
  IKEv1 SA: local 22.1.12.1/500 remote 22.1.23.3/500 Active
  Session ID: 0
  IKEv1 SA: local 22.1.12.1/500 remote 22.1.23.3/500 Active
  IPSEC FLOW: permit 47 host 22.1.12.1 host 22.1.23.3
        Active SAs: 4, origin: crypto map
```

More interestingly, we'd like to check spoke-to-spoke tunnels are protected by IPSec.

R3 and R5 both have two sets of isakmp SAs, to the Hub router and to each other directly.

```
R3#show crypto isakmp sa
```

R3 and R5 both have two sets of isakmp SAs, to the Hub router and to each other directly.

```
R3#show crypto isakmp sa
IPv4 Crypto ISAKMP SA
dst             src             state           conn-id status
22.1.12.1       22.1.23.3       QM_IDLE            1001 ACTIVE
22.1.23.3       22.1.12.1       QM_IDLE            1004 ACTIVE
22.1.23.3       22.1.25.5       QM_IDLE            1003 ACTIVE
22.1.25.5       22.1.23.3       QM_IDLE            1002 ACTIVE

R5#show crypto isakmp sa
IPv4 Crypto ISAKMP SA
dst             src             state           conn-id status
22.1.25.5       22.1.12.1       QM_IDLE            1002 ACTIVE
22.1.23.3       22.1.25.5       QM_IDLE            1004 ACTIVE
22.1.25.5       22.1.23.3       QM_IDLE            1003 ACTIVE
22.1.12.1       22.1.25.5       QM_IDLE            1001 ACTIVE
```

Additionally, let's verify the traffic is actually encrypted by the crypto we configured. On R5 use "show crypto ipsec sa" to see "encaps" and "decaps" traffic. The "encaps" and "decaps" counters show how many packets have been processed through the IPSec crypto machine. When a ping (ICMP) packet is sent from R5 to R3, it first gets encrypted by R5 and then decrypted by R3. The return traffic will trigger the "decaps" counter. So, if we sent 5 ping packets from R5 to R3, we are expecting to see the counters to increment on both routers. If the counters do not change while ping is working, we can tell the traffic did not get IPSec encryption while traversing the network.

`R5#show crypto ipsec sa`

```
R5#show crypto ipsec sa

interface: Tunnel0
   Crypto map tag: Tunnel0-head-0, local addr 22.1.25.5

  protected vrf: (none)
  local  ident (addr/mask/prot/port): (22.1.25.5/255.255.255.255/47/0)
  remote ident (addr/mask/prot/port): (22.1.23.3/255.255.255.255/47/0)
  current_peer 22.1.23.3 port 500
    PERMIT, flags={origin_is_acl,}
   #pkts encaps: 5, #pkts encrypt: 5, #pkts digest: 5
   #pkts decaps: 5, #pkts decrypt: 5, #pkts verify: 5
   #pkts compressed: 0, #pkts decompressed: 0
   #pkts not compressed: 0, #pkts compr. failed: 0
   #pkts not decompressed: 0, #pkts decompress failed: 0
   #send errors 0, #recv errors 0
```

On R5, ping R3 over DMVPN tunnel. 5 icmp packets were sent.

```
R5#ping 10.1.1.3
Type escape sequence to abort.
Sending 5, 100-byte ICMP Echos to 10.1.1.3, timeout is 2 seconds:
!!!!!
Success rate is 100 percent (5/5), round-trip min/avg/max = 15/17/22 ms
```

We have verified the DMVPN is working. The final step is to encrypt the tunnel traffic with IPSec. Exam the "encaps" and "decaps" counter.

```
R5#show crypto ipsec sa

interface: Tunnel0
    Crypto map tag: Tunnel0-head-0, local addr 22.1.25.5

   protected vrf: (none)
   local  ident (addr/mask/prot/port): (22.1.25.5/255.255.255.255/47/0)
   remote ident (addr/mask/prot/port): (22.1.23.3/255.255.255.255/47/0)
   current_peer 22.1.23.3 port 500
     PERMIT, flags={origin_is_acl,}
    #pkts encaps: 10, #pkts encrypt: 10, #pkts digest: 10
    #pkts decaps: 10, #pkts decrypt: 10, #pkts verify: 10
    #pkts compressed: 0, #pkts decompressed: 0
    #pkts not compressed: 0, #pkts compr. failed: 0
    #pkts not decompressed: 0, #pkts decompress failed: 0
    #send errors 0, #recv errors 0
```

We have confirmed that the traffic sending across DMVPN tunnels are encrypted by IPsec. Congratulations, you have completed this topology.

Topology 9: Configuring MPLS VPN, VRF, OSPF and BGP

Overview

Multi-Protocol Label Switching (MPLS) is a method of packet forwarding on the network. Packets are labelled with one or more labels. As each packet passes through the MPLS network, labels may be added, replaced or stripped off. The network distributes information so that each switch knows what it is supposed to do if it encounters a particular label.

When used with MPLS, the VPN feature allows several sites to interconnect transparently through a service provider's network. One service provider network can support several different IP VPNs. Each of these appears to its users as a private network, separate from all other networks. Within a VPN, each site can send IP packets to any other site in the same VPN.

Each VPN is associated with one or more VPN routing or forwarding instances (VRFs). A VRF consists of an IP routing table, a derived Cisco express forwarding (CEF) table, and a set of interfaces that use this forwarding table. These are the acronyms that often used:

- P (Provider) routers are ISP core routers which don't connect to customer routers
- PE (Provider Edge) routers connect to Customer Edge (CE) as a handoff point.
- CE (Customer Edge) routers exist at the edge of a customer site.

Network Topology

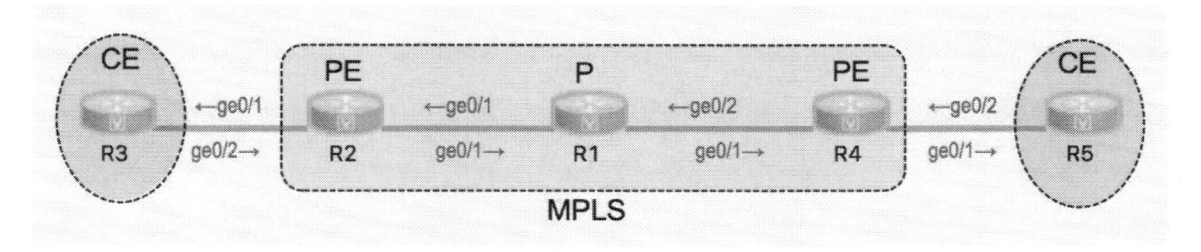

The network topology includes five routers. R1, R2 and R4 are Provider routers and R3 and R5 are customer CE Routers. What has been done in the initial configuration:

- Wiring among the switches and routers
- Host names
- OOB management IP addresses
- Username / Password for switches and routers: cisco / cisco

Requirements

1. R1 is the P (Provider) core router. R2 and R4 are PE (Provider Edge) routers connected to R3 and R5. R3 and R5 are CE (Customer Edge) routers. The goal is to build a Layer 3 MPLS link between customer branch offices R3 and R5.
2. Configure MPLS on R1, R2 and R4, enable LDP label exchange. Always use the router's Loopback0 interface as source for LDP sessions with password VIRLBOOK.
3. Assign a unique VRF named SNS to the customer. Configure BGP VPN between R1, R2 and R4. R1 shall serve as route reflector.
4. Enable OSPF routing between PE and CE routers. Both R3 and R5 shall belong to OSPF area 0.
5. As results, a Layer 3 MPLS VPN is established for the customer. R3 and R5 (and their internal networks) shall have full access to each other's networks.

Solutions

1. Configure IGP (OSPF) among provider routers, enable MPLS on provider backbone.

Provider backbone routers need to be able to reach each other freely. We configured OSPF among R1, R2 and R4.

```
!R1
router ospf 1
 router-id 1.1.1.1
 network 1.1.1.1 0.0.0.0 area 0
 network 22.1.0.0 0.0.255.255 area 0
!
!R2
router ospf 1
 router-id 2.2.2.2
 network 2.2.2.2 0.0.0.0 area 0
 network 22.1.0.0 0.0.255.255 area 0
!
!R4
router ospf 1
 router-id 4.4.4.4
 network 4.4.4.4 0.0.0.0 area 0
 network 22.1.0.0 0.0.255.255 area 0
!
```

Verify the OSPF neighbors are up on R1, R2 and R4. And they can ping each other.

```
R1#sho ip ospf nei

Neighbor ID     Pri   State         Dead Time   Address       Interface
4.4.4.4           1   FULL/DR       00:00:39    22.1.14.4     GigabitEthernet0/2
2.2.2.2           1   FULL/DR       00:00:37    22.1.12.2     GigabitEthernet0/1
```

Enabling MPLS interfaces with "mpls ip" command. Note that MPLS is not enabled on the customer facing interfaces. LDP is the default label distribution protocol. We need to make sure always use Loopback interface to form LDP relationships because Loopback interfaces never go down. We'll also protect the peering sessions by using a password.

```
!R1
mpls ldp password required
mpls ldp neighbor 2.2.2.2 password VIRLBOOK
mpls ldp neighbor 4.4.4.4 password VIRLBOOK
!
mpls ldp router-id Loopback0
!
interface range GigabitEthernet0/1,2
 mpls ip
end

!R2
mpls ldp router-id Loopback0
access-list 10 permit 2.2.2.2
!
mpls ldp password required
mpls ldp neighbor 1.1.1.1 password VIRLBOOK
no mpls ldp advertise-labels
mpls ldp advertise-labels for 10
!
interface GigabitEthernet0/1
 mpls ip
end

!R4
mpls ldp router-id Loopback0
access-list 10 permit 4.4.4.4
!
mpls ldp password required
mpls ldp neighbor 1.1.1.1 password VIRLBOOK
no mpls ldp advertise-labels
mpls ldp advertise-labels for 10
!
interface GigabitEthernet0/1
```

```
 mpls ip
end
```

Verify R1 has LDP peering relationship with R2 and R4.

`R1#show mpls ldp neighbor`

```
R1#show mpls ldp neighbor
    Peer LDP Ident: 2.2.2.2:0; Local LDP Ident 1.1.1.1:0
        TCP connection: 2.2.2.2.35593 - 1.1.1.1.646
        State: Oper; Msgs sent/rcvd: 105/100; Downstream
        Up time: 01:25:15
        LDP discovery sources:
          GigabitEthernet0/1, Src IP addr: 22.1.12.2
        Addresses bound to peer LDP Ident:
          2.2.2.2        22.1.12.2
    Peer LDP Ident: 4.4.4.4:0; Local LDP Ident 1.1.1.1:0
        TCP connection: 4.4.4.4.21589 - 1.1.1.1.646
        State: Oper; Msgs sent/rcvd: 106/102; Downstream
        Up time: 01:25:15
        LDP discovery sources:
          GigabitEthernet0/2, Src IP addr: 22.1.14.4
        Addresses bound to peer LDP Ident:
          4.4.4.4        22.1.14.4
```

Confirm LDP authentication is required and password is in use.

`R1#show mpls ldp neighbor password`

```
R1#show mpls ldp neighbor password
    Peer LDP Ident: 2.2.2.2:0; Local LDP Ident 1.1.1.1:0
        TCP connection: 2.2.2.2.35593 - 1.1.1.1.646
        Password: required, neighbor, in use
        State: Oper; Msgs sent/rcvd: 108/103
    Peer LDP Ident: 4.4.4.4:0; Local LDP Ident 1.1.1.1:0
        TCP connection: 4.4.4.4.21589 - 1.1.1.1.646
        Password: required, neighbor, in use
        State: Oper; Msgs sent/rcvd: 109/105
```

2. Create and assign a unique VRF to the customer

In this step, we create customer VRFs on our PE routers and assign the customer-facing interfaces to them. We need to assign each VRF a route distinguisher (RD) to uniquely identify prefixes as belonging to that VRF and one or more route targets

(RTs) to specify how routes should be imported to and exported from the VRF. A route distinguisher for each VRF in the form of XX:YY. Only customer facing PE routers would need the VRF configuration.

```
!R2
vrf definition SNS
 rd 2.2.2.2:1
 route-target import 200:200
 !
 address-family ipv4
  export map EXPORT
 exit-address-family
!
interface GigabitEthernet0/2
 description to R3
 vrf forwarding SNS
!
route-map EXPORT permit 10
 set extcommunity rt 100:100
!
```

```
!R4
vrf definition SNS
 rd 4.4.4.4:1
 route-target import 100:100
 !
 address-family ipv4
  export map EXPORT
 exit-address-family
!
interface GigabitEthernet0/2
 description to R5
 vrf forwarding SNS
!
route-map EXPORT permit 10
 set extcommunity rt 200:200
!
```

Verify VRF interfaces and VFR status.

```
R2#show ip vrf interfaces
R2#show vrf
```

On R2, Gig0/2 is the VRF "SNS" interface we created. The other "Mgmt-intf" VRF is the default management VRF comes with the router's initial configuration.

```
R2#show ip vrf interfaces
Interface              IP-Address      VRF                              Protocol
Gi0/0                  172.16.1.164    Mgmt-intf                        up
Gi0/2                  192.168.1.2     SNS                              up
R2#
R2#show vrf
  Name                                 Default RD       Protocols   Interfaces
  Mgmt-intf                            <not set>        ipv4,ipv6   Gi0/0
  SNS                                  2.2.2.2:1        ipv4        Gi0/2
```

Next step is to configure MP-BGP among provider routers to help exchange customer routes.

3. Configure MP-BGP between PE routers and use R1 as route reflector.

In order to carry VRF customer routes inside provider's network, multiprotocol BGP (MP-BGP) must be used. Each VRF operates on its own routing domain. MP-BGP runs only on the PE routers. The P router (R1) is not aware of the VRF operations. Configure BGP on provider routers R1, R2 and R4. In addition to the VPNv4 address family, address families for the the customer VRF SNS have been created. Support for extended community strings has been added to the VPNv4 neighbor configuration.

```
!R1
router bgp 65300
 bgp log-neighbor-changes
 no bgp default ipv4-unicast
 neighbor BGPPEERS peer-group
 neighbor BGPPEERS remote-as 65300
 neighbor BGPPEERS update-source Loopback0
 neighbor 2.2.2.2 peer-group BGPPEERS
 neighbor 4.4.4.4 peer-group BGPPEERS
 !
 address-family ipv4
  neighbor BGPPEERS route-reflector-client
  neighbor 2.2.2.2 activate
  neighbor 4.4.4.4 activate
 exit-address-family
 !
 address-family vpnv4
  neighbor BGPPEERS send-community extended
  neighbor BGPPEERS route-reflector-client
  neighbor 2.2.2.2 activate
  neighbor 4.4.4.4 activate
 exit-address-family
```

```
!R2
router bgp 65300
 bgp log-neighbor-changes
 no bgp default ipv4-unicast
 neighbor 1.1.1.1 remote-as 65300
 neighbor 1.1.1.1 update-source Loopback0
 !
 address-family ipv4
  neighbor 1.1.1.1 activate
 exit-address-family
 !
 address-family vpnv4
  neighbor 1.1.1.1 activate
  neighbor 1.1.1.1 send-community extended
 exit-address-family
 !
 address-family ipv4 vrf SNS
 exit-address-family
 !

!R4
router bgp 65300
 bgp log-neighbor-changes
 no bgp default ipv4-unicast
 neighbor 1.1.1.1 remote-as 65300
 neighbor 1.1.1.1 update-source Loopback0
 !
 address-family ipv4
  neighbor 1.1.1.1 activate
 exit-address-family
 !
 address-family vpnv4
  neighbor 1.1.1.1 activate
  neighbor 1.1.1.1 send-community extended
 exit-address-family
 !
 address-family ipv4 vrf SNS
 exit-address-family
 !
```

Verify R1, R2 and R4 have formed BGP relationship.

```
R1#show ip bgp summary
```

```
R1#show ip bgp summary
BGP router identifier 1.1.1.1, local AS number 65300
BGP table version is 1, main routing table version 1

Neighbor        V          AS MsgRcvd MsgSent   TblVer  InQ OutQ Up/Down  State/PfxRcd
2.2.2.2         4       65300     138     143        1    0    0 02:01:52           0
4.4.4.4         4       65300     139     144        1    0    0 02:01:51           0
```

4. Enable OSPF routing between PE and CE routers. R3 and R5 shall belong to OSPF area 0.

Note this would be the secondary OSPF routing process on the PE routers. Don't get confused. "router ospf 1" was configured for the provider network so R1, R2 and R4 can reach each other. "router ospf 2" is to only peer with the CE router and carry in customer prefixes. The PE router will package the customer prefixes and ship them over the BGP backbone to the other end of the CE router of the same customer. Two OSPF processes work independently.

```
!R2
router ospf 2 vrf SNS
!
interface GigabitEthernet0/2
 ip ospf 2 area 0
end

!R4
router ospf 2 vrf SNS
!
interface GigabitEthernet0/2
 ip ospf 2 area 0
end
```

Customer routers only have standard and simple OSPF configuration.

```
!R3
router ospf 1
 router-id 3.3.3.3
 network 3.3.3.3 0.0.0.0 area 0
 network 192.168.1.3 0.0.0.0 area 0
!
!R5
router ospf 1
 router-id 5.5.5.5
 network 5.5.5.5 0.0.0.0 area 0
 network 10.1.1.5 0.0.0.0 area 0
!
```

```
R3,R5#show ip ospf neighbor
```

```
R3#show ip ospf neighbor

Neighbor ID     Pri   State        Dead Time   Address       Interface
192.168.1.2      1    FULL/DR      00:00:33    192.168.1.2   GigabitEthernet0/1
```
```
R5#show ip ospf neighbor

Neighbor ID     Pri   State        Dead Time   Address       Interface
10.1.1.4         1    FULL/DR      00:00:36    10.1.1.4      GigabitEthernet0/1
```

The final step is to mutually redistribute routes between OSPF and BGP on the PE routers.

5. Enable route redistribution between the customer sites and the provider router.

Without redistribution, provider routers would not be able to transport the customer routes to the other end of the customer network. Redistribution is typically done on the PE routers to inject customer routes into MPLS VPN. And the other hand, it is handed off to the PE router to tell the local OSPF router about the customer routes. It is done through redistribution as well.

```
!R2
router bgp 65300
...
address-family ipv4 vrf SNS
  redistribute ospf 2
 exit-address-family
!
router ospf 2 vrf SNS
 redistribute bgp 65300 subnets
!

!R4
router bgp 65300
...
address-family ipv4 vrf SNS
  redistribute ospf 2
 exit-address-family
!
router ospf 2 vrf SNS
 redistribute bgp 65300 subnets
!
```

The goal of the routing protocol redistribution between OSPF and BGP on the PE routers are:

- Tell its backbone BGP about what it has learned about its side of the customer network. For example, from R2's perspective, it'll learn everything about what the CE router R3 had to tell it and send the information to its BGP peer R1. When you have multiple customers, they'll be put in their own VRF and VPN so they have their own routing domain and perfectly isolated.
- On the other direction, the PE router also tells the CE router about what it knows in its BGP table about the same customer that the provider learned from the other side of the customer network.
- With PE and P routers' help, the provider has setup a perfectly isolated routing information exchange board dedicated to this customer.

Let's take a look at what R2 has learned from the customer (R3).

```
R2#show ip route vrf SNS bgp
```

```
R2#show ip route vrf SNS bgp

Routing Table: SNS
Codes: L - local, C - connected, S - static, R - RIP, M - mobile, B - BGP
       D - EIGRP, EX - EIGRP external, O - OSPF, IA - OSPF inter area
       N1 - OSPF NSSA external type 1, N2 - OSPF NSSA external type 2
       E1 - OSPF external type 1, E2 - OSPF external type 2
       i - IS-IS, su - IS-IS summary, L1 - IS-IS level-1, L2 - IS-IS level-2
       ia - IS-IS inter area, * - candidate default, U - per-user static route
       o - ODR, P - periodic downloaded static route, H - NHRP, l - LISP
       a - application route
       + - replicated route, % - next hop override, p - overrides from PfR

Gateway of last resort is not set

      5.0.0.0/32 is subnetted, 1 subnets
B        5.5.5.5 [200/2] via 4.4.4.4, 02:51:40
      10.0.0.0/24 is subnetted, 1 subnets
B        10.1.1.0 [200/0] via 4.4.4.4, 02:51:40
```

R2 has learned about R5's loopback IP address 5.5.5.5 and the local network connected to R5 (10.1.1.0/24). What about R4?

```
R4#show ip route vrf SNS bgp

Routing Table: SNS
Codes: L - local, C - connected, S - static, R - RIP, M - mobile, B - BGP
       D - EIGRP, EX - EIGRP external, O - OSPF, IA - OSPF inter area
       N1 - OSPF NSSA external type 1, N2 - OSPF NSSA external type 2
       E1 - OSPF external type 1, E2 - OSPF external type 2
       i - IS-IS, su - IS-IS summary, L1 - IS-IS level-1, L2 - IS-IS level-2
       ia - IS-IS inter area, * - candidate default, U - per-user static route
       o - ODR, P - periodic downloaded static route, H - NHRP, l - LISP
       a - application route
       + - replicated route, % - next hop override, p - overrides from PfR

Gateway of last resort is not set

      3.0.0.0/32 is subnetted, 1 subnets
B        3.3.3.3 [200/2] via 2.2.2.2, 02:54:12
B     192.168.1.0/24 [200/0] via 2.2.2.2, 02:54:12
```

R4 has learned about R3. It's loopback address 3.3.3.3 and the local network 192.168.1.0/24. Now the provider knows both end of the customer networks and all it needs to do is to share it with the other end. Once done that, both end of the customer networks can reach each other via the provider's network.

On the CE routers, they learn the network via standard OSPF. Let's see what we have in their routing tables.

```
R3,R5#show ip route
```

```
         3.0.0.0/32 is subnetted, 1 subnets
C           3.3.3.3 is directly connected, Loopback0
         5.0.0.0/32 is subnetted, 1 subnets
O IA        5.5.5.5 [110/3] via 192.168.1.2, 03:00:19, GigabitEthernet0/1
         10.0.0.0/24 is subnetted, 1 subnets
O IA        10.1.1.0 [110/2] via 192.168.1.2, 03:00:19, GigabitEthernet0/1
         192.168.1.0/24 is variably subnetted, 2 subnets, 2 masks
C           192.168.1.0/24 is directly connected, GigabitEthernet0/1
L           192.168.1.3/32 is directly connected, GigabitEthernet0/1
R3#
```

```
         3.0.0.0/32 is subnetted, 1 subnets
O IA     3.3.3.3 [110/3] via 10.1.1.4, 03:02:14, GigabitEthernet0/1
         5.0.0.0/32 is subnetted, 1 subnets
C           5.5.5.5 is directly connected, Loopback0
         10.0.0.0/8 is variably subnetted, 2 subnets, 2 masks
C           10.1.1.0/24 is directly connected, GigabitEthernet0/1
L           10.1.1.5/32 is directly connected, GigabitEthernet0/1
O IA     192.168.1.0/24 [110/2] via 10.1.1.4, 03:02:14, GigabitEthernet0/1
R5#
```

R3 and R5 have routes for each other and they should be able to ping each other.

```
R3#ping 5.5.5.5
R3#traceroute 5.5.5.5
```

```
R3#ping 5.5.5.5
Type escape sequence to abort.
Sending 5, 100-byte ICMP Echos to 5.5.5.5, timeout is 2 seconds:
!!!!!
Success rate is 100 percent (5/5), round-trip min/avg/max = 5/7/12 ms
```

```
R3#traceroute 5.5.5.5
Type escape sequence to abort.
Tracing the route to 5.5.5.5
VRF info: (vrf in name/id, vrf out name/id)
  1 192.168.1.2 4 msec 4 msec 3 msec
  2 22.1.12.1 [MPLS: Labels 16/19 Exp 0] 8 msec 6 msec 8 msec
  3 10.1.1.4 [MPLS: Label 19 Exp 0] 5 msec 8 msec 5 msec
  4 10.1.1.5 7 msec *  6 msec
R3#
```

Traceroute indicates the traffic is going through a MPLS VPN.

```
R5#ping 3.3.3.3
R5#traceroute 3.3.3.3
```

```
R5#ping 3.3.3.3
Type escape sequence to abort.
Sending 5, 100-byte ICMP Echos to 3.3.3.3, timeout is 2 seconds:
!!!!!
Success rate is 100 percent (5/5), round-trip min/avg/max = 3/7/15 ms
R5#
R5#traceroute 3.3.3.3
Type escape sequence to abort.
Tracing the route to 3.3.3.3
VRF info: (vrf in name/id, vrf out name/id)
  1 10.1.1.4 6 msec 6 msec 3 msec
  2 22.1.14.1 [MPLS: Labels 17/19 Exp 0] 12 msec 7 msec 6 msec
  3 192.168.1.2 [MPLS: Label 19 Exp 0] 6 msec 8 msec 6 msec
  4 192.168.1.3 5 msec *  9 msec
R5#
```

You can also check the MPLS forwarding table on those MPLS enabled provider routers.

```
R2#show mpls forwarding-table
```

```
R2#show mpls forwarding-table
Local    Outgoing    Prefix            Bytes Label    Outgoing       Next Hop
Label    Label       or Tunnel Id      Switched       interface
16       16          4.4.4.4/32        0              Gi0/1          22.1.12.1
17       Pop Label   1.1.1.1/32        0              Gi0/1          22.1.12.1
18       Pop Label   22.1.14.0/24      0              Gi0/1          22.1.12.1
19       No Label    3.3.3.3/32[V]     1254           Gi0/2          192.168.1.3
20       No Label    192.168.1.0/24[V] \
                                       1814           aggregate/SNS
```

R4#show mpls forwarding-table

```
R4#show mpls forwarding-table
Local    Outgoing    Prefix            Bytes Label    Outgoing       Next Hop
Label    Label       or Tunnel Id      Switched       interface
16       17          2.2.2.2/32        0              Gi0/1          22.1.14.1
17       Pop Label   1.1.1.1/32        0              Gi0/1          22.1.14.1
18       Pop Label   22.1.12.0/24      0              Gi0/1          22.1.14.1
19       No Label    5.5.5.5/32[V]     1254           Gi0/2          10.1.1.5
20       No Label    10.1.1.0/24[V]    1814           aggregate/SNS
R4#
```

We have validated that a layer 3 MPLS VPN has been built for this customer and the customer routers R3 and R5 have full access to each other's networks.

Appendix A: Using External Telnet SSH Clients

For those who prefer using their own Telnet/SSH client such as SecureCRT and Putty (for Mac users, iTerm2 or the built-in Terminal), you may configure your system to use the Telnet/SSH client you prefer to connect to a virtual router. The terminal window that comes with VM Maestro is not as intuitive and customizable as other widely popular clients, such as SecureCRT, Putty and iTerm2 for Mac.

VM Maestro provides the option of using external terminal programs. First, we need to understand how to call those programs in command line.

Putty

Find out the path where the executable file (putty.exe) is located. The easiest way is open Windows Explore and search for "putty.exe" on your C: or on whatever hard drive volume you installed the application. For me, it is located at "C:\Program Files (x86)\PuTTY\putty.exe". Open VM Maestro and go to Files – Preferences. Select Cisco Terminal and go to Use external terminal applications.

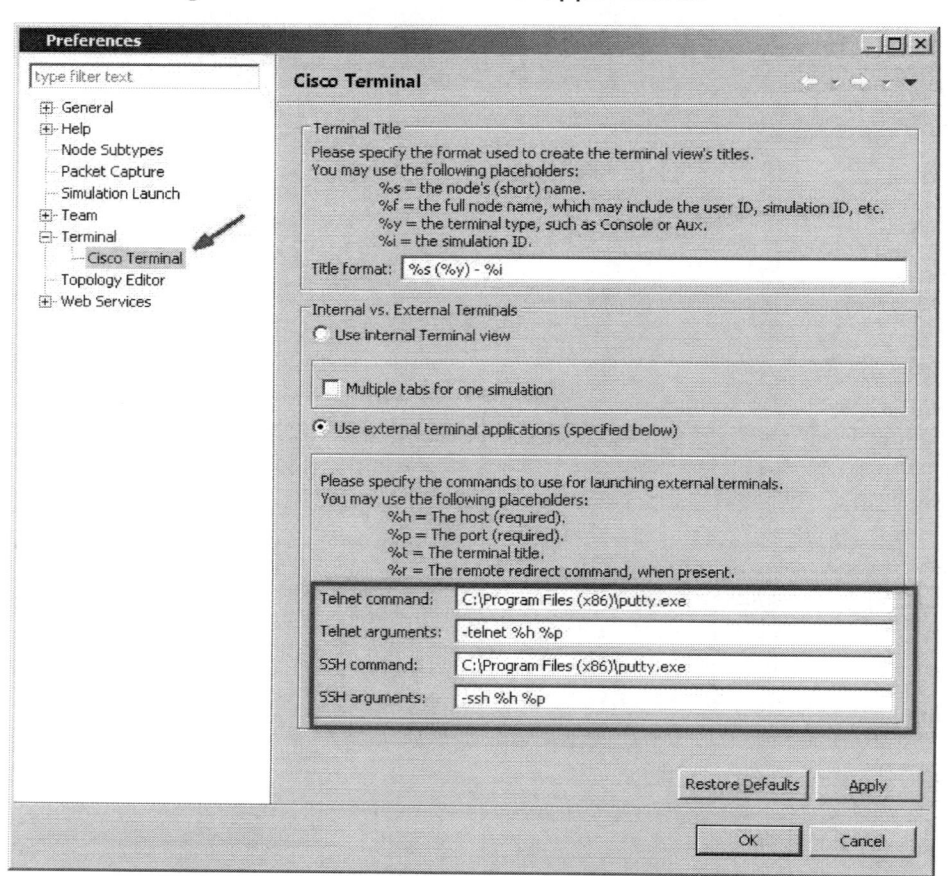

Here is an example and what each parameter means.

```
Telnet Command: C:\Program Files (x86)\PuTTY\putty.exe
Telnet Argument: -telnet %h %p
SSH Command: C:\Program Files (x86)\PuTTY\putty.exe

SSH Setting: -ssh %h %p
%h specifies the host to connect to (required)
%p specifies the port to connect to (required)
%t the title of your terminal client (optional)
%r the remote redirect command (optional)
```

Secure CRT

Similarly, find the path to SecureCRT.exe. In my environment it is at: "C:\Program Files\VanDyke Software\SecureCRT\SecureCRT.exe". Put the following string into the Telnet and SSH command boxes:

```
Telnet commend:
C:\Program Files\VanDyke Software\SecureCRT\SecureCRT.exe
Telnet Argument: /N %t /T /TELNET %h %p
SSH commend:
C:\Program Files\VanDyke Software\SecureCRT\SecureCRT.exe
SSH Argument /N %t /T /SSH %h %p
The /T option ensures Secure CRT creates a tab for new sessions,
instead of opening a new window.
The /N option sets the tab's title based on the title format string.
Make sure to validate / adapt the path of the binary.
```

Now every time you right click on a simulated network node and open the Console port, your external terminal program Putty or SecureCRT will be launched instead.

For Mac users, I'll pick the most commonly used built-in terminal client and the free 3rdparty iTerm2 as examples. Unlike in the Windows environment where you can call an external application from Maestro directly, in Mac OS we'll have to use an Apple Script to call iTerm2 or Terminal. The overall process is rather simple, except you call a Script from Maestro instead calling the terminal application directly. Open the Apple Script Editor. If you have never used it before, just search for it in Spotlight Search.

Mac OS X Built-in Terminal

Copy and paste the code below in the Script Editor and save file format as "script".

```
on run argv
        tell application "Terminal"
            activate
            -- open a new Tab, sadly, there is no method
            tell application "System Events"
                keystroke "t" using {command down}
            end tell
            repeat with win in windows
                try
                    if get frontmost of win is true then
                        set cmd to "/usr/bin/" & item 1 of argv &
" " & item 2 of argv & " " & item 3 of argv
                        do script cmd in (selected tab of win)
                        set custom title of (selected tab of win)
to
item 4 of argv
                    end if
                end try
            end repeat
        end tell
end run
```

Mac OS X iTerm2

Copy and paste the code below in the Script Editor and save file format as "script".

```
on run argv
        -- last argument should be the window title
        set windowtitle to item (the count of argv) of argv as text
        -- all but last argument go into CLI parameters
        set cliargs to ""
        repeat with arg in items 1 thru -2 of argv
            set cliargs to cliargs & " " & arg as text
        end repeat
        tell application "iTerm"
          activate
          tell current window
                set newTab to (create tab with default profile)
                tell the current session of newTab
                    set name to windowtitle
                    write text cliargs
                end tell
          end tell
```

```
        end tell
end run
```

After you saved the script, you may call it from VM Maestro client. Make sure you use the correct path to point to the script you just saved. You can use the Linux command "pwd" (stands for print working directory) and "ls" to verify the path. In my case, it is located at:

```
/Users/username/virl-iterm2.scpt
```

Change your path accordingly. Here is the format you are going to put in VM Maestro client. Don't change anything else other than the path to your script.

```
Telnet Command: /Usr/bin/osascript
Telnet Arguments:/Users/username/virl-iterm2.scpt telnet %h %p %t

SSH Command:  /Usr/bin/osascript
SSH Arguments: /Users/username/virl-iterm2.scpt ssh -Atp%p guest@%h %r %t
```

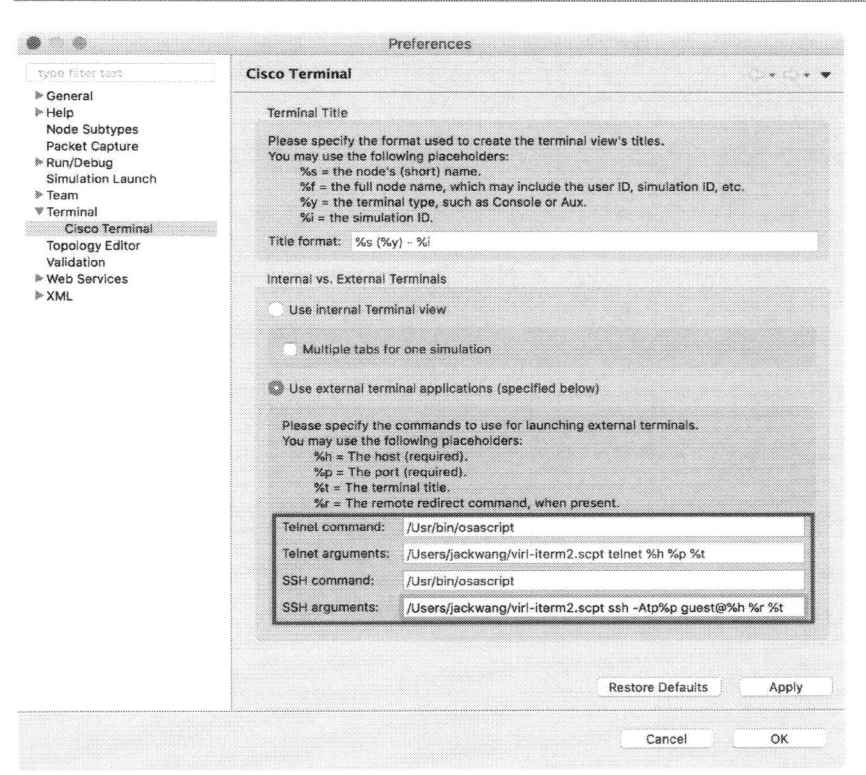

Now when you open a Telnet session to a node's Console port, it will open the terminal client you configured. Tab tiles display the host names nicely.

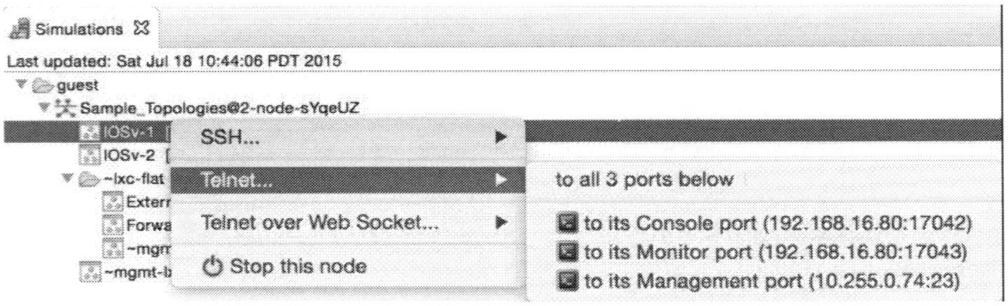
Simulations
Last updated: Sat Jul 18 10:44:06 PDT 2015
guest
Sample_Topologies@2-node-sYqeUZ
IOSv-1
IOSv-2
~lxc-flat
SSH...
Telnet...
Telnet over Web Socket...
Stop this node
to all 3 ports below
to its Console port (192.168.16.80:17042)
to its Monitor port (192.168.16.80:17043)
to its Management port (10.255.0.74:23)

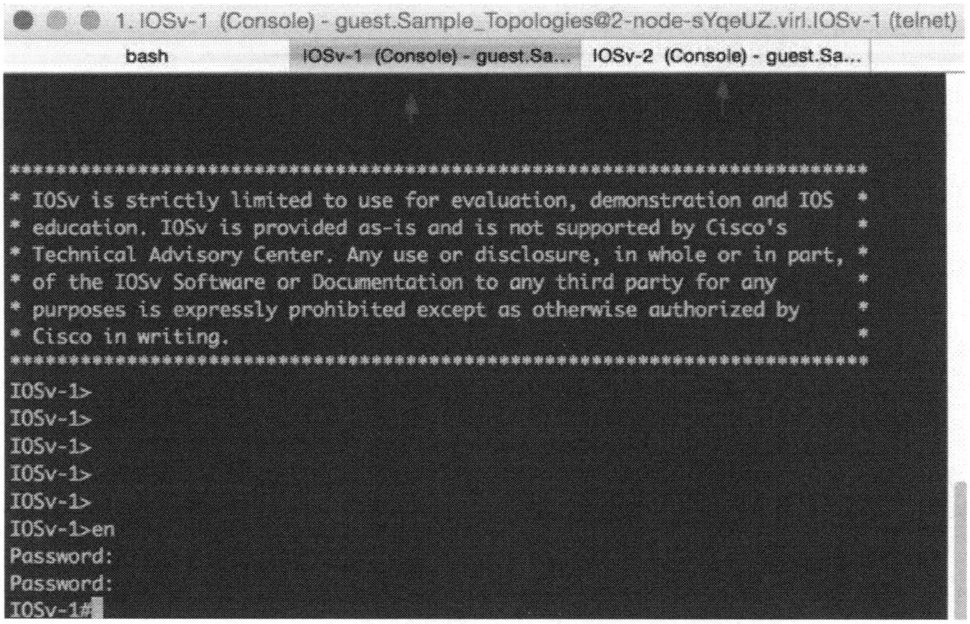
1. IOSv-1 (Console) - guest.Sample_Topologies@2-node-sYqeUZ.virl.IOSv-1 (telnet)
bash
IOSv-1 (Console) - guest.Sa...
IOSv-2 (Console) - guest.Sa...
* IOSv is strictly limited to use for evaluation, demonstration and IOS *
* education. IOSv is provided as-is and is not supported by Cisco's *
* Technical Advisory Center. Any use or disclosure, in whole or in part, *
* of the IOSv Software or Documentation to any third party for any *
* purposes is expressly prohibited except as otherwise authorized by *
* Cisco in writing. *
IOSv-1>
IOSv-1>en
Password:
IOSv-1#

Appendix B: Node Naming and IP Addressing Scheme

The workbook follows certain node naming convention and IP addressing scheme. By following these rules, you no longer need to memorize or lookup the IP address of any routers or switches. It will save you time and help you put more energy towards learning the technology, rather than looking up for IP addresses.

Node Naming

We always use "R1", "R2"… for routers, "SW1", "SW2"… for switches, "FW1", "FW2"… for ASAv firewalls and "PC1", "PC2"… for servers.

IPv4 Addressing

For loopback addresses, a node uses its own number with a /32 subnet mask. For example, R1's Loopback IP address is 1.1.1.1/32 and R2's Loopback IP address is 2.2.2.2/32, and so on.

For inter-node connections, we use 22.1.XX.YY /24 block.

For the first two octets ("22.1." in my example), you can use any numbers as long as they compose a valid IP address. Since we are working in a lab environment, private or public IP ranges do not matter. My general recommendations are as follows. First make it easy to type on the keyboard. Consider that you'll have to type the IP address in CLI every time you Ping or Traceroute, do routing table lookups and so on. Secondly, you can use the second octet to separate students into groups if you are an instructor. For example, Group A would use 22.1.XX.YY /16 and Group B would use 22.2.XX.YY /16 for the labs.

I use the third octet "XX" to indicate to whom am I connecting. And the forth octet "YY" indicates my own node number. This is best explained with an example. For instance, R1 is directly connected with R2. I would give R1 an IP address 22.1.12.1 /24 and R2 an IP address 22.1.12.2 /24. The third octet "12" states, we are connected between R1 and R2. It always starts with the smaller number first. The forth octet "1" is for R1 and "2" is for R2. Here is a quick example to help you to put all the pieces together.

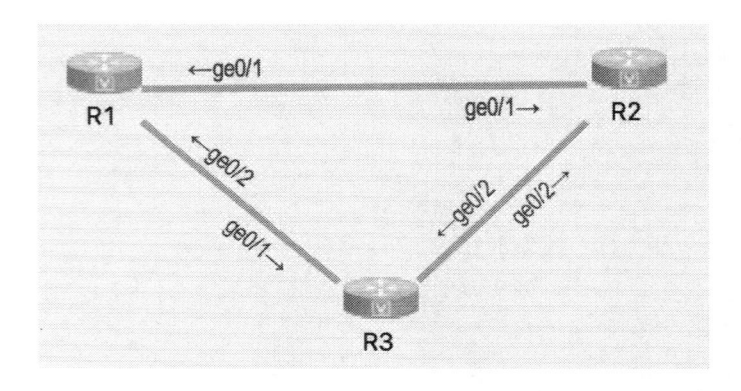

```
R1:
Loopback 1.1.1.1 /32
Gig0/1: 22.1.12.1 /24
Gig0/2: 22.1.13.1 /24

R2:
Loopback 2.2.2.2 /32
Gig0/1: 22.1.12.2 /24
Gig0/2: 22.1.23.2 /24

R3:
Loopback 3.3.3.3 /32
Gig0/1: 22.1.13.3 /24
Gig0/2: 22.1.23.3 /24
```

What about switches? Assuming we won't be running more than 19 IOSv routers at the same time, I simply add a "2" in front of the switch number for switch IPs. For example, SW1's loopback address would be 21.21.21.21/32. When R1 is connected with SW1, the IP address on the R1 side would be 22.1.121.1 /24. The SVI IP address on SW1 would be 22.1.121.21 /24. It only matters when we treat the switch as a Layer 3 device and let it participate in routing. If the switch is only used as Layer 2, you don't need to worry about SVI IP addresses. As long as the hosts are connected to the switch ports that are on the same VLAN, hosts can communicate to each other. The switch does not participate in routing.

IPv6 Addressing

Understanding how we came up with the IPv4 IP addressing scheme, IPv6 is simple. It is just a numbering game where we try to make the IP addresses make sense while not breaking the rules. An IPv6 address is represented as eight groups of four hexadecimal digits, each group representing 16 bits (two octets). One group of consecutive zero values may be replaced with a single empty group of two consecutive colons (::).

For IPv6 loopback addresses, we came up from its IPv4 address and prepending the first 16-bit block with a /128 mask. For example, R1's IPv6 loopback address is 2001:1:1:1::1 /128 and R2's Loopback IP address is 2001:2:2:2::2 /128. And so on…

For inter-node connections, we use 2001:22:1:XX::YY /64 block. Knowing how the IPv6 scheme was designed, you know what router interface has what IP address. We also inherited some of the IPv4 addressing ideas. Given the same example above, their IPv6 addresses are as following:

```
R1:
Loopback 2001:1:1:1::1/128
Gig0/1: 2001:22:1:12::1 /64
Gig0/2: 2001:22:1:13::1 /64

R2:
Loopback 2001:2:2:2::2 /32
Gig0/1: 2001:22:1:12::2 /24
Gig0/2: 2001:22:1:23::2 /24

R3:
Loopback 2001:3:3:3::3 /32
Gig0/1: 2001:22:1:13::3 /24
Gig0/2: 2001:22:1:23::3 /24
```

Why we are doing all the IP numbering conventions? It is because we try to make the IP addressing follow certain rules so that we know what IP address to expect on an interface without memorizing or looking it up. It will save you a tremendous amount of time when working on a large and complex CCIE lab.

Appendix C: Recommended Reading

The Cisco VIRL BOOK

Cisco Virtual Internet Routing Lab (VIRL) is a software tool to build and run network simulations without the need for physical hardware. The VIRL Book guides you through installing, configuring and using VIRL on Windows, Mac OSX, VMware ESXi and Cloud environments.

The book is written for students who are studying for CCNA, CCNP and CCIE certification exams, training and learning about network technologies. This book is also for IT networking professionals who want to mock up production network, test network changes, and new features without risking downtime. Book URL: www.virlbook.com